A Call for Economic Nationalism:

How Globalization And Deindustrialization Turned The American Dream Into A Nightmare

* *

Vanzetti Vandal

Vandal Brothers, LLC

2016

First edition.

Released March 1, 2016.

Published by Vandal Brothers, LLC

Bath, Ohio. USA.

ISBN: 978-1-944149-01-7

For more information, news, and to contact the author, visit:

www.vandalvoid.com

Contents

Foreword

Today, just sixteen years into the twenty-first century, the American working and middling classes find themselves in an increasingly precarious position. The dual threats of immigration and deindustrialization—two sides of the same globalist coin—continue to threaten the standard of living and the quality of life of the average American. In a trend that has been occurring since the 1970's, American manufacturing jobs have been increasingly outsourced overseas, leaving lower-paying and often part time service jobs as the only real option for the uneducated. And the liberal immigration policies that began with the 1965 Immigration and Nationality Act have only served to keep these jobs low-paying by flooding the labor market with cheap immigrant labor. For a while, the educated had a refuge in the growing tech industry, but foreign workers have been increasingly imported to supplant American tech workers via H-1B visas. Thus, American workers of all stripes increasingly find themselves between a rock and a hard place. And that is where *A Call For Economic Nationalism* comes into play.

My brother, Vanzetti Vandal, has done a brilliant and highly commendable job in this book of researching, analyzing, and presenting both the history as well as the continued workings of these unfortunate phenomena—deindustrialization via outsourcing, wage stagnation due to mass immigration, and worker replacement via visa programs. And in doing so, he has done a great service to his fellow Americans, who all feel but are often unable to articulate or even understand these phenomena fully. The most unsettling aspects, to me, of these above phenomena are twofold. Firstly, that such policies have and continue to be actively promoted by literally all the leaders and politicians of both major political parties. And secondly, that these policies have continued so long without the greater American populace grasping what has been going on and mounting a concerted effort to save the fortunes of their shared nation. That is, hopefully, until now.

The contemporary campaign of candidate Donald J. Trump is perhaps representative of the first real and promising revolt of the average American citizen, We the People, against the corrupt elites of both parties and their disastrous policies, which have placed us in this increasingly precarious economic position. There are many facets to Trump's appeal; however, there are two issues in particular that have set him apart from all the other candidates (and all contemporary American politicians in general). These are the issues of trade and immigration.

The bulk of Trump's supporters is composed of the victims of deindustrialization. They are the average Americans who have been left behind by joint schemes of politicians, international financiers, and multinational corporations who have all colluded to outsource American manufacturing jobs overseas in order to cut labor costs. Trump has promised the American people that he will, not only end this gutting of America's industry, but also reverse it. He has spoken about the idiotic refusal of the United States to simply tax foreign manufactures the same exact way that every single other nation on Earth does—an unfair situation, which is mostly to blame for the slow death of American industry. And he has promised to end this idiocy via the implementation of tariffs that tax foreign manufactures, so that the United States may simply become—just like every other developed or developing nation on Earth—capable of protecting its own economy, industry, and workers.

Trump has also made immigration a key aspect of his campaign. The promise to, not only build a wall along the Mexican border, but also deport all and any illegal immigrants that are already living in the country has endeared him to the white working class, whose members justifiably view the leniency of authorities and politicians towards such illegal immigrants resentfully. Although Trump has not yet come out in opposition to legal immigration, which Vanzetti has shown in this book is just as harmful as illegal immigration, he has proposed to temporarily ban the most volatile and unassimilable immigrants—that is, Muslim immigrants—from even entering the country. And Trump has caught a lot of heat for staking out these politically incorrect positions. But he has not backed down against the entire elite apparatus that has come down in full force upon him. Thus, middle America rightfully and increasingly views Trump as the only viable hope for making our nation great again—a rebellious hero who will finally slay the twin devils of deindustrialization and immigration.

And there is indeed precedent for We the People standing up and reversing the suicidal policies of our traitorous elites. In the case of immigration, during the late nineteenth and early twentieth centuries, America's political and business elites had colluded to keep the borders of the United States wide open against the will of the American people. This was all done in order to permit the influx of cheap immigrant labor, which was utilized as a bludgeon against the American working class, which was desperately trying to unionize and demand concessions from the robber barons who subjected them to horrendously low wages and harsh working conditions. However, with the passage of the 1924 National Origins Act, the American lower and middling classes had succeeded in putting an end to such liberal immigration policies. From that point onward, minus setbacks caused by the worldwide depression of the 1930's, the American standard of living and quality of life continued to increase as an American labor shortage forced businesses to make concessions to the American worker. Of course, the resultant prosperity allowed We the People to become complacent, and Lyndon Baines Johnson succeeded in reviving liberal immigration policies with the 1965 Immigration and Nationality Act.

So there is hope for We the People. We have stopped our traitorous elites before, and if Trump wins this November, we just may be able to stop them again. And that is perhaps why this book is so important. So few Americans really understand the phenomena that are currently imperiling the American economy. We the People need to spread this understanding if we are ever to be successful in saving the inheritance of our born and unborn American children and grandchildren. When you are done reading this book, give it to a friend or family member. These are desperate times, and only a great union of will and concert of action can save us. This year's election may very well prove to be the last desperate chance that We the People will have to preserve what once was the greatest country that the world has ever known.

Sacco Vandal

February 16, 2016

Introduction

Deindustrialization: Good or bad?

Deindustrialization and its relation to globalization is a very difficult and complicated phenomenon. Even though there have been diverse scholarly and popular accounts of the subject, most Americans struggle to understand these broad and far reaching developments. Some studies point to the benefits of deindustrialization and welcome the advent of a post-industrial society. Other studies lament the decline of the factory system. There remains no general consensus, and each American has tried to piece together an understanding based on assumptions that they have imbibed. The point of this study is to try and make sense of such assumptions, to determine whether they have been beneficial or detrimental to Americans and America as a whole, and to offer up a prescription that will secure the future prosperity of the United States.

Three different stories from personal interviews with average Americans from the heart of the midwest rust belt, Ohio, illustrate the broad effects of deindustrialization and globalization on the American worker. Each respective opinion is directly related to their working experience and how their careers have been affected by deindustrialization. Thomas Fenske has spent an entire career working in the automobile industry. He started back in the 1970s when American car manufacturers still dominated in the United States. Fenske sternly asserts that American car companies were producing sub-par products. As a service adviser, he witnessed brand new cars whose hoods would not close evenly, improperly installed transmissions, and cars that would not align. He says that American manufacturers "put out crap and no one did anything because of the unions... the Japanese came over and they figured this out, there wasn't any quality." Fenske believes the uncompetitiveness of American car manufacturers was caused by the auto workers' union and the Environmental Protection Agency's (EPA) regulations, which allowed the Japanese to get a foothold in the American market. "It was the unions and the EPA requirements that pushed this overseas. A corporation is a living breathing thing that will survive whether or not you push it overseas, they will move it overseas."

However, it is not necessarily the pay and benefits of unions that Fenske attributes to the downfall of the auto industry, but the work rules. When he worked at the Ford plant, Fenske recalls that the millwrights could not use a certain grade of tin without calling in the tinners. They could not work with a heavier grade of steel than they were allowed because the tinners would file a grievance. Rules of this nature are meant to prevent workers from doing another union member's job, but they hurt efficiency. Fenske explains that one side of the plant was for sales and one side was manufacturing, and whenever he tried to pick up parts on the sales side the manufacturers were not allowed to move the parts because it was someone else's work. He says that the company "lost work and people lost their job because we couldn't do someone else's job. It's frustrating because work stops until we let everyone do their job. It's not the wages, it's the work rules. I can't do that because it's someone else's job. You're crippling the employer. To do one job, you need four people." Fenske believes that none of these work rules help the workers, but are in place only to create union dues because each additional worker pays dues. He claims that when Walmart came into communities that the union would pay people to picket. He also claims that a man who owned a meat store in Medina, Ohio, paid union dues for the meat cutters' union even though he was not a member of the union, but paid merely so the union would not picket his store. Fenske believes that this shows that the unions do not care about the workers. He says that it is about "the dues and more money. If the Union really cared about the worker, then they would cut the dues in half and let the worker bring home more money. Why should the elected members of the union make more money than the rank and file that they came from?"

However, Thomas Fenske is not in manufacturing, but in sales. He has no vested interest in American car manufacturers because he just sells parts, regardless of where they are manufactured. He admits that he is "selling from what's on the road already. It doesn't matter where the parts are made. They're sent to us every night, some of it's made here, some of it's made there, some of it's made in Mexico...it comes from all over the world. You have to get the parts from somewhere, parts are parts." Fenske's view towards deindustrialization follows the mainstream Republican narrative.[1] He believes that greedy unions and government regulations are at fault. Nonetheless, he has no problem buying foreign cars because he believes they are of better quality at a better price. He believes in the free market and free trade. Nevertheless, his career has not been negatively affected by deindustrialization or globalization.

Brian Waller is more critical of free trade, globalization, and deindustrialization, likely because his career has been adversely affected by these developments. Waller is a draftsman; however, even though he is a white collar worker, his career has been just as vulnerable to deindustrialization as many blue collar careers in manufacturing. As Ohio has gone through deindustrialization, he says he has watched all the talent leave. "Who's gonna be flocking to Ohio? The talent pool isn't here so the work I do isn't around here anymore. I could have moved to Phoenix when it was booming and got a job, but there's no work in Ohio." Without the necessary talent in a specific field being present in Ohio, it is difficult for businesses to get started in that field. And when there is work around, it is usually only temporary. When Waller got out of high school in 1979, he says that he could get a decent paying job anywhere he wanted and expect to retire from that job with a pension. However, he says that throughout his lifetime he has watched that change.

Throughout the 1980's, Waller found himself getting laid off again and again. During the boom years, he had plenty of work, but every time there was a recession he would get laid off. By the

1990's, Waller found himself working as a temporary contractor. "No healthcare, no benefits. I wasn't an employee, just a contractor. The companies started implementing flex teams so that they could just bring people in on contract for six months at a time. You can't go and work for a company and retire from it. Everything is flex teams." Around the same time, computers and the internet allowed for an unprecedented level of global integration that allowed companies to outsource white collar jobs like Waller's. He says "you can e-mail blueprints around the world. Someone in India or China can do all the work and just one American engineer has to check the work. The work I used to be doing was already done in China. You can hire a draftsman cheaper in China than to hire Brian Waller. White collar workers have been affected by the internet. Everything is done on computers." For the next fifteen years, Waller continued to work temporary jobs as a contractor, jumping from company to company. But by 2007 he was only making $15 an hour, whereas he was making $17.50 an hour ten years earlier. His wages were shrinking and it was becoming increasingly difficult to secure new contracts. Then the Great Recession hit. Waller explains the increasingly precarious position that deindustrialization and other global economic trends were putting him in:

> In January 2009 I got laid off indefinitely. I haven't been called back, I did what I was supposed to do and put in resumes, but who's gonna talk to a fifty year old compared to

> a young kid right out of school or foreigners? It was futile; after over 2 years of putting in resumes and my unemployment running out I just gave up. Since then it's taken its toll on my psyche. I'm just fed up with this country. I'm not gonna go bust my ass at Walmart or McDonald's when I'm over fifty years old. I've already had a heart attack. I would either drop dead or kill some idiot that I would have to deal with. It would be impossible for me. I could show up for a week or two and try to be cheery, but then I would snap and say fuck this, throw the burgers down, and walk out before I hurt somebody. With my experience and skills, I should be making over twenty-dollars an hour in my field. I haven't given up, but I have nothing to give to some company that cares nothing about my well-being. You get hired on contract temporary work for so long and then you're gone the second they don't need you. I have nothing left to give.

Waller can recall a time in the 1980's when he worked for a company that treated him like family. He made decent money, had good health coverage, and paid vacations. The boss was genuinely worried when he was sick, and every Christmas he would give out bonuses so that his employees could buy gifts for their family. It was a small sized company that was not obsessed with growth or with pleasing investors, but was mainly concerned with its employees.

Waller believes that corporate, government, and union greed are all responsible for deindustrialization, and that companies no longer care about their employees.

Similarly, Eric Anderson has been a blue collar worker for 28 years. He works in manufacturing in the steelworkers union. In the early 2000's, financial troubles led to the plant he works at becoming "worker operated" to prevent a shut down. Part of the buyout contract that was worked out with investors included a two dollar per hour pay cut and a seven year pay freeze. The workers were also guaranteed profit sharing, but Anderson says that "they never followed through. A CEO was hired who went in the wrong direction and we lost out. But his contract guaranteed him $5 million a year and we had to pay him." After that, a multinational conglomerate out of New Zealand bought out the company in order to strip its assets. Anderson claims that they were "planning on coming in, stripping the company, and selling off the parts. But they haven't done it yet because their buyers backed out. They're still planning on selling off the company even though we're profitable." The new parent conglomerate has not been updating their machinery or investing back in the company, but they are still purchasing other companies. It is just a matter of time before the plant gets shut down.

Like Waller, Anderson attributes deindustrialization to greed. He views the outsourcing of jobs and manufacturing overseas as being motivated by greed. Despite these convictions, Anderson is not a champion of unions. He says, "to work there, I gotta be in the union, but they've never done anything for me. My union dues don't go towards my retirement, the company pays that, but our pension is broke. We got a letter saying that the union invested our retirement wrong. They said the fund pool is getting smaller, so we're not gonna get what we paid into...they say we're gonna get 60% but they might be facing bankruptcy and then we won't get anything. I've showed up and done my job, that's what gives me job security, not the union." Anderson has worked 50 to 60 hours a week on swing shift for almost thirty years. He only stayed at the company because he thought he could rely on the pension, but the union invested the money with investment banks and lost it during the financial crisis of 2008-9.

Most people would attribute deindustrialization to some form of greed, unless they themselves have benefited from the phenomenon. One of the purposes of this study is to analyze who benefits and who loses from deindustrialization and globalization. The other purposes of this study is to determine who and what has caused deindustrialization and what America must do to reverse it. In order to understand deindustrialization, one must research the policies, institutions, and individuals that have caused deindustrialization. The role that politicians have played, along with how their policies have contributed to deindustrialization, and whether they have been working in the best interests of the American people or global elites, needs to be examined. How international financiers on Wall Street and the corporate greed of multinational corporations have encouraged deindustrialization must be explored. The unions also need to be investigated in order to see how they have undermined competitiveness, and so does the effects of environmental regulations. How globalization and the liberalization of immigration policy affects the wages and job opportunities of American workers needs to be given a brazenly serious analysis. This study will be conducted free of any political correctness.

In chapter one, deindustrialization and its effects on the average worker is examined (with a focus on the Midwest United States). Chapter two focuses on the automobile industry by using the struggle of the Fisher Body Division of General Motors in Cleveland, Ohio, as a case study. Chapter three takes a look at the steel industry by focusing on the strife of Youngstown, Ohio, and Republic Steel in particular. Chapter four documents the policies and factors that have been fueling deindustrialization throughout America and that still continue up until today. And chapter five highlights the detrimental consequences of lax immigration policies, and makes a case for a nationally coordinated policy to reverse deindustrialization that places America and Americans first. There are countless examples that could be examined in order to better understand deindustrialization. This study focuses mainly on Fisher Body Company and Republic Steel as examples to demonstrate the phenomenon of deindustrialization because they are two local cases whose struggle can easily be juxtaposed to demonstrate the cases of multiple other companies that have also been faced with the peril of deindustrialization. Keep in mind that this study is meant to deal with the issue of deindustrialization on a national level and to treat the United States as an international player affected by globalization.

Deindustrialization of the Heartland

The Future of the U.S.

Throughout the developed world globalization has had varied effects. Globalization has created distinct winners and losers, certain nations benefitting and others facing great difficulties. Some nations have witnessed the decline of manufacturing, and other nations have been industrializing at a rapid pace. Some individuals have benefited from the decline of manufacturing, while other individuals have suffered great losses. The post-industrial age is a term that is often used by those who view the decline in manufacturing as a positive phenomenon. Those who view the decline of manufacturing as a negative phenomenon tend to prefer the term deindustrialization. The post-industrial camp heralds the creation of a superior and more-evolved era that will be defined by high-tech industries and a prosperous service economy. The critics of deindustrialization argue that the loss of large numbers of well-paid manufacturing jobs has destroyed the middle class and widened the gap between the rich and the poor. Regardless of the interpretation, there is no denying that the decline in manufacturing has caused a massive loss of industrial jobs.[2]

Whether an American uses the term post-industrial age or deindustrialization, one thing remains evident: The current economic trends seem to portend dire consequences for the entire nation. There is a widening gap between the rich and the poor. The national debt is over twenty trillion dollars and climbing. The annual trade deficit is over five-hundred billion dollars and there are no signs that this trend will be reversed. American is the largest debtor nation in the world, and that debt is held by countries who are rivals of America. Real wages in America have been steadily declining. The real unemployment rate is well over fifteen percent. The middle class is smaller than ever and shrinking. Vital industries to national security have been outsourced to potential enemies of America, such as China. And our elected representatives seem unable to effectively address such problems, except with the same old prescriptions that have created such disastrous results in the first place.[3]

In order to fully grasp the current situation, one must first look to the decline of manufacturing in the traditional heartland of American industry, the Midwest, in the last third of the twentieth century.

The Rise and Fall of the American Heartland

The Midwest has traditionally produced the majority of America's metals, machinery, consumer and producer durables, and a large portion of the nation's agriculture. This area is comprised of the five states of Ohio, Michigan, Indiana, Illinois, and Wisconsin. These states are bordered by the Great Lakes to the north, the Appalachian Mountains to the east, the Mississippi River to the west, and the Ohio River to the south. This network of rivers and the proximity of the Great Lakes encouraged the construction of canals, which—along with railroads and steamboats—allowed for efficient transportation that fueled industrial development in the region during the antebellum period. Ann R. Markusen and Virginia Carlson define the Midwest as thus:[4]

> A region tied together by such waterways as the Great Lakes, and the Ohio, Mississippi, and Missouri River systems, its original cohesiveness developed during the water transportation era. In the mid-19th century, as water transportation gave way to rail, the interrelationships were cemented through a vast internal trading pattern in which the more easterly areas supplied steel, machinery, farm implements, and household goods for the more westerly areas. The latter paid for these manufactured goods with abundant agricultural produce and other resource-based commodities such as timber and iron ore.[5]

From 1835 until 1945, this region was largely shielded from recessions and proved to be an extremely robust economy, based primarily on large machine industries, such as machinery, metals, and consumer and producer durables.[6]

In the decades after World War I, deindustrialization began in New England, but was more slow paced and not as severe as the deindustrialization that would take place in the Midwest during the 1970's and the 1980's. Michigan and Ohio were hit the hardest by deindustrialization, but the region as a whole has suffered from higher unemployment rates than the national average and a net population loss due to out-migration. Those leaving were largely college graduates and skilled blue-collar workers who pursued better career opportunities in the Sunbelt, a term that refers to the American South and Southwest. Michigan and Ohio together lost more than 125,000 in population from 1980-85 alone, whereas the Sunbelt states gained on average a five percent increase in population during the same period. In the aftermath of World War II America had begun a shift towards the electronic and aerospace industries, and these industries were overwhelmingly concentrated in the Sunbelt This shift was the beginning of a greater trend towards high tech industry and the advent of a post-industrial age for America.[7]

The fact that this region is generally warmer and receives more sunshine is why it is referred to as the Sunbelt, but the term is also used to denote the growth in industry and population in the second half of the twentieth century. Before the New Deal the South and Southwest were largely undeveloped regions. During the 1930's the federal government funded water and power projects that transformed the region's infrastructure and economy. At the same time, private businessmen and other professionals encouraged investment in economic diversification. But it was World War II that had the largest impact on modernizing and industrializing the South and Southwest. President Roosevelt sought to disperse war production throughout America's interior for defense purposes and to aid in economic development. Billions of dollars were allocated to new military bases and war production plants in the region. Fears about post-war decline led to a concerted effort to attract industry to the Sunbelt. To create a business friendly environment, government at the local and state level pursued policies of tax breaks and land grants, and passed right-to-work legislation. Many of these efforts attracted businesses from the Midwest; however, defense and tech industries have become the prime economic engine throughout the Sunbelt because they have established a comparative advantage in those industries.[8]

A comparative advantage is when one region or country can produce a specific product the cheapest and most efficiently. Generally, they export this product to other countries or regions and import products that can be made cheaper and more efficiently elsewhere. Certain individuals who look towards the post-industrial age with optimism will often explain deindustrialization as a natural, benign phenomenon where comparative advantage shifts. Among those who advocate for free-market-capitalism and free trade are individuals who believe that the "invisible hand" will sort everything out for the better in the long-run; however, many of these individuals are the ones who benefit from free trade because they work in the industries and sectors in which the United States has a comparative advantage. The internationalization of markets gives the United States a comparative advantage in arms, electronics, pharmaceuticals, business services, and the entertainment industry. This advantage in services is due to U.S. primacy in banks, financial exchanges, law firms, accountants, and large capitalist institutions like the World Bank and the International Monetary Fund. Other sectors of the economy, such as consumer goods, consumer durables, and non-military capital goods, which utilize low-skilled laborers, suffer from competition from the developed and developing world. Countries that are less developed than the United States have a comparative advantage in industries that utilize low-skilled workers because the labor is cheaper; therefore, free trade would naturally cause low-skilled jobs to be exported to where labor is cheapest. But defense and related industries would grow and prosper in this region commonly referred to as the Sunbelt.[9]

Markusen and Carlson assert that the term "Sunbelt" is not sufficient. They prefer to use the term "defense perimeter," which stretches from New England down to Florida, through Texas and the South West and up the West Coast through Washington and to

Alaska. The jobs in this region were fueled by the United States' defense industry, which became a permanent industrial complex after World War II. A majority of defense industry jobs focused on research and development, design, high-tech electronics, and guidance systems. The defense industry fueled many of these high-tech jobs, but they operated in smaller orders of higher priced unites. A fighter jet or a missile is more labor-intensive than an automobile. Thus, the industry of the Sunbelt is in stark contrast with the mass-production found in much of the Midwest industries. The Midwest did not have very good incentives to get in on the military-industrial complex early on because it already had a well-established industrial base. Additionally, the Midwest states were more politically divided than the Sunbelt, which prevented statewide coordinated efforts to accommodate defense oriented industries. The defense perimeter states sent politicians to Washington to lobby for the construction of military facilities and contracts, but no coordinated effort ever arose from the politicians of the Midwest.[10]

In the Midwest, the steel, auto, farm machinery, and railroad equipment industries easily held a long period of dominance in their markets; thus, leaders of these industries worried more about preserving their market shares and stabilizing competition instead of investing in product innovation. Bad restructuring decisions in the scramble to deal with foreign competition has caused mergers, buyouts, and diversification and costly legal fees that further hurt these already injured industries. The replacement of the Midwest's manufacturing with foreign imports has devastated the region economically, but no one has suffered more than those individuals who worked in these industries. The decline of manufacturing in the Midwest led to large numbers of displaced workers who found it extremely difficult to find new employment in a changing economic environment.[11]

Workers, Their Families, and Their Communities

According to Barry Bluestone and Bennett Harrison, evidence for the social impact of deindustrialization was hidden during the 1970's in Gross National Product (GNP) figures and inaccurate and impersonal unemployment numbers. The GNP represents the dollar value of all the goods and services produced in the country; thus, a high GNP does not directly correlate to the industrial strength of the United States because "services" that produce nothing are incorporated into the figures. The unemployment figures are likewise misleading in gauging economic well-being because they discount anyone who is not actively searching for a job or who has dropped out of the workforce due to disillusionment. Large percentages of displaced workers have trouble finding new employment and even when they do the loss of seniority makes any job prospects less secure with lower status and lower wages. Three-fifths of displaced workers undergo decreased occupational status, and the downward mobility is often the most severe for professionals and managerial workers. Being laid off or being displaced by deindustrialization is not a temporary loss because most workers take many years to recover, and a significant number never recover the income or status that they lost. Besides income, displaced workers lose health insurance for themselves and their families, and they also lose part or all of their pensions. Families can weather brief periods of lay offs by surviving on savings and unemployment insurance, but when someone is permanently laid off, then their family often loses all of their accumulated assets.[12]

Although the loss of material wealth is devastating to a family in itself, the loss of this wealth alone is not the only problem facing the families of displaced workers. In a 1984 op-ed piece in the *Washington Post*, Mark Shields noted that deindustrialization is a human tragedy that entails, not only the loss of income, but the loss of status and self-esteem as well. Merely measuring a family's loss in dollar amounts and economic terms fails to take into account the whole spectrum of misfortunes that befalls the family of a permanently displaced worker. Severe economic distress is responsible for a vast array of health problems, both physical and mental. Studies show that displaced workers suffer from increased blood pressure, high cholesterol and blood glucose levels, which result in higher risks of heart disease. They also are more susceptible to ulcers, respiratory diseases, and hyper-allergic reactions due to stress, diabetes, and gout. Of course some of these diseases could be due to poor nutrition and the curtailment of health care; however, higher rates of recurring headaches, upset stomachs, depression, increased aggression, anxiety, and alcohol abuse are common among displaced workers. Many of these health problems can be demonstrated in the results from interviews of 200 displaced workers from Pratt & Whitney, a jet engine company, in the mid 1980's that showed how the unemployed workers from the plant suffered from chronic insomnia, headaches, and stomach ailments that were caused by personal and family tensions due to income insecurity.[13]

More startling are the figures that show an increase in deaths from homicides, suicides, and heart failure among displaced workers. There are also increased levels of admittance to prisons and mental hospitals for these workers. Dr. Harvey Brenner of Johns Hopkins University statistically correlated a mere 1% rise is aggregate unemployment over 6 years with 920 suicides, 650 homicides, 500 cirrhoses of the liver, 4,000 admissions to mental hospitals, and 3,300 incarcerations. Often it is the case that when an individual loses his/her job they also lose their social networks, and frustration over prolonged periods of unemployment and isolation leads to a decrease in self-esteem, which often strains family relations and causes an increase in child abuse and spousal abuse.[14]

These problems facing the displaced worker are often made worse by an individual's conviction that his/her misfortunes are the result of their own personal failings. It does not help that American society views economic deprivation as some sort of moral shortcoming; thus, the displaced worker, who is the victim of deindustrialization, is often blamed for their economic loss as some sign of their own moral or personal failings, which generates a cycle of destruction that is hard to break free from. Each failed attempt to acquire a new job reinforces the stigma that there is something inherently morally wrong with the displaced worker and that they deserve their misfortune.[15]

These problems facing workers who have been displaced

by deindustrialization become compounded because it is never just a few random workers and their families that are affected, but whole communities are displaced when plants shut down their operations. Many communities throughout the Midwest have been historically dependent on specific manufacturing industries. In many cases, the community itself was erected specifically to meet the labor demands of these local manufacturing industries. It is difficult to ascertain how Detroit would have developed into such a massive urban center without the automotive industry, and the decline of the automotive industry in Detroit has displaced thousands of industrial workers and caused a mass exodus of its population. Detroit, the capital of the American auto-industry, has witnessed the evaporation of the majority of its auto plants since its heyday in the 1950's. The city has lost countless jobs, fallen victim to massive emigration, and witnessed the disintegration of its public services. The city's population has plummeted from a peak of 1.8 million inhabitants to roughly 700,000 in 2010. The loss of property tax and income tax on such a massive scale forced the city to declare bankruptcy in 2013.[16]

Likewise, Youngstown, Ohio, located in the Mahoning Valley, or the "Steel Valley", became the epicenter of the steel industry. In Youngstown, during the 1970s and 1980s, the decline of the American steel industry had catastrophic consequences for, not only the steel workers, but the entire greater community and regional economy as well. Even the solvency of municipal governments can be thrown into jeopardy as their largest tax base dries up, which is what happened to Detroit when the city declared bankruptcy. Youngstown was able to avoid bankruptcy, but it still faced severe economic strain due to the loss of taxes associated with the steel industry that reverberated through all levels of government. In the first thirty-nine months after the closing of the Youngstown Sheet and Tube plant, the surrounding communities lost $8 million in taxes. The county lost an additional $1 million, the state lost $8 million, and the federal government lost $15 million, which totals $32 million in lost tax revenues. In the bordering town of Campbell, where the Youngstown Sheet and Tube Company was located, over half a million dollars from individual income taxes and $130,000 in annual property taxes was lost.[17]

Government financial problems do not end with the loss of tax bases. Compounding their woes was an increase in social welfare spending to meet the needs of the large numbers of displaced workers. Due to the closing of Youngstown Sheet and Tube, the tax revenues were reduced while public expenditure was increased. In Youngstown, the loss of $32 million in tax revenue from the closing of mills coincided with an increased expenditure of $38 million for Trade Readjustment Assistance (TRA), which is a federal program that provides services to those affected by foreign imports. Thus, the costs of the shutdown reached a combined total of $70 million, but the real loss was undoubtedly higher. There were countless other businesses that lost revenue or went out of business themselves from the sudden loss of Youngstown Sheet and Tube's business or its former employees as customers. The closing of Youngstown Sheet and Tube Company was just the beginning of the community's troubles.[18]

Other industrial centers, such as Cleveland, Ohio were created, not merely to sustain one specific industry, but instead to serve as centers for multiple industries because of their location. Cleveland's position on Lake Erie allowed the city to utilize the water systems and canals to establish itself as the hub of the Great Lakes maritime trade system. Being the epicenter of the Great Lakes trade routes enabled Cleveland to develop extensively in many industries, including auto, steel, oil, and heavy equipment. Unfortunately, Cleveland—like Youngstown and Detroit—has been hit extremely hard by deindustrialization. Between 1950 and 1990, Cleveland lost nearly 140,000 industrial jobs, and the city's population decreased by over 400,000 from its peak of over 900,000 in 1950.[19]

An excellent example to highlight the deindustrialization of Cleveland can be witnessed in the case of the General Motors' Fisher Body plants on Coit Road and Euclid. In regards to the closing of GM's Fisher Body plants in the Cleveland area, Dr. James Q. Aylesworth, an economics professor at Lakeland Community College in Kirtland, said that "Everyone will be affected. Small businesses like tool and die businesses, will be hurt. Businesses that sell luxury items like clothing will be hurt. Service industries will be hurt. It goes on and on...It devastates the economy in much the same way cancer destroys the human body—slowly." He went on to say that the GM plants employed over 4,000 employees and did business with 658 and 298 businesses within a 50-mile radius, respectively. These companies made bearings, screws, steel, power presses, hydraulic fluids and foams, tool and die makers that were used at the Coit Road Euclid plants. Due to the shutdowns these companies lost $38.5 million in business. The banks were also hurt and foreclosures surrounding the displaced workers increased. Just as Keynesian economics relies on the multiplier effect for every dollar of government spending to fuel economic prosperity, the loss of every dollar from the economy has a multiplier effect that causes economic devastation and fuels recession.[20]

This domino effect associated with the decline of manufacturing and the negative effect it has on those communities has been articulated best by Barry Bluestone and Bennett Harrison in their article, *The Deindustrialization of America.* They wrote:

> The unit's own employees lose salaries and wages, pensions, and other fringe benefits; supplier firms lose contracts; and the various levels of government lose corporate income and commercial property tax revenue. These in turn result in a series of secondary shocks including decreased retail purchases in the community, a reduction in earnings at supplier plants, and increased unemployment in other sectors. Finally, these events produce tertiary effects in the form of

> increased demand for public assistance and social services, reduced personal tax receipts, and eventually layoffs in other industries, including the public sector. What begins as a behind-closed-doors company decision to shut down a particular production facility ends up affecting literally everyone in town, including the butcher, the baker, and the candlestick maker. By the time all of these 'ripple effects' spread throughout the economy, workers and families far removed from the original plant closing can be affected, often with dramatic consequences.[21]

Any plant closing will have a multiplier effect on the community that is many times more than the immediately displaced employees, especially if the industry that shuts down is a purchaser of other goods and services produced by other businesses, and if they are a major employer. For example, in the case of the closing of the Youngstown Sheet and Tube plant there were 4,100 immediately displaced steelworkers, but a Policy Management Associates study concluded that the closing caused a further displacement of 12,000 to 13,000 other workers and curtailed retail sales in the community by $12 to $23 million per year. Not only did the private sector suffer devastating losses, but the estimated $70 million cost to government in lost tax revenue and increased expenditure failed to take in an even bigger cost that included the businesses and workers dependent on the business of Youngstown Sheet and Tube and its employees.

Social and fiscal burdens will then lead to the cutting of public expenditure, which makes city, county, and state employees also vulnerable to unemployment during the time their services are needed most.[22]

The Post-Industrial Society

Post-industrial advocates rationalize these as growing pains in the transition to a post-industrial society that will replace the old order with a brighter and more prosperous economy. Those who support global free trade have argued that "any industry that needed protection did not deserve to exist," and "that displaced workers could simply find jobs in other areas of the economy." [23] However, it is difficult for large segments of displaced workers to find adequate work and start over, and many of these victims of deindustrialization have lost their self-respect, their dignity, and their houses. But advocates of the post-industrial age believe that tech and service jobs will offer new opportunities that will be more beneficial for the American workforce.[24]

It is true that service and other jobs are being created to replace the jobs lost in the manufacturing sector. Between 1950 and 1990, manufacturing jobs fell from 38.9% of total jobs in the United States to 21.6%. At the same time, service and finance jobs increased from 17.5% to 37.1%. However, the bulk of the jobs created were far below the earning potential of the manufacturing jobs that they replaced. The average industrial job earned $22,000 in 1984, where the average service job only earned $12,500 and offered 15 percent fewer hours. This situation caused workers to work two or three jobs just to stay in the middle class. If every displaced industrial worker is forced to take on two service jobs just to match his previous income, then there needs to be two service jobs created for every manufacturing job lost. This prospect can be very difficult considering that as manufacturing jobs are lost, the community also suffers a loss of service jobs due to the negative impact of the multiplier effect.[25]

As for the tech industries there has been significant growth, but the wages in this sector are extremely uneven and have helped to codify an increasing gap between the classes. There has only been a small number of professional jobs created that pay well, whereas the vast majority of the jobs created either are at or barely above the minimum wage level. According to Katherine S. Newman, "More than half of the eight-million (net) new jobs created in the United States between 1979 and 1984 paid less than $7,000 per year (in 1984 dollars). While many of these were part-time jobs (another growth area of dubious value), more than 20 percent of the year-round, full-time jobs created during this period paid no more than $7,000."[26] It would seem that the transition to a post-industrial society entails an increasingly huge disparity between economic classes. Not only do many of the new jobs in the service sector pay significantly less, but they also fail to offer many of the benefits that define a union job in manufacturing. Due to this "pyramidal" job growth, "which features small numbers of good jobs compared to large numbers of bad jobs," the United States is becoming more polarized via an increasing distinction between haves and have nots.[27]

Although many of the jobs that have been lost were of a manufacturing or blue collar nature, many white collar workers have also suffered from deindustrialization. Both blue collar and white collar workers have suffered from displacement due to the decline in manufacturing, and those that have not lost their jobs or those that have found new jobs have suffered wage cuts. However, certain highly educated individuals have actually benefitted from globalization and deindustrialization. Peter Gottschalk and Mary Joyce in a study showed that greater inequality in the United States is due to "increases in trade, declines in manufacturing, and increases in service sector jobs."[28] Their study further documents that "highly educated workers, who were already receiving above-average wages in the 1970's, received substantial raises during the 1980s. At the other end of the spectrum, high school dropouts and high school graduates experienced actual declines in pay."[29] Thus, foreign competition led to a shift from demand for unskilled workers in the U.S. to a demand for high-skilled workers, which widened the gap of inequality. Only individuals in fields such as finance have benefited. Contrariwise, the American dream has failed for individuals who believed that through hard work alone that they could have earned a decent living and could have improved their lot in life, and it has also failed for many who have pursued higher education in the hopes of working their way up the corporate ladder.[30]

In the economic boom after World War II, upward mobility could be taken for granted. Because earnings were on the rise for all workers, no matter an individual's education or job, workers could advance economically just by working the same job their entire life. Americans have always viewed economic success as linked to individual effort and connected it to the morality of the individual, regardless of greater economic trends. The "American Dream" tells a person that if they work hard they will succeed and acquire happiness. The post-war boom of three decades of wage growth made everyone believe that just by working hard that they were entitled to middle-class lifestyles. A middle aged industrial worker who loses his job to a plant closing also loses the seniority that his life had been structured upon. Seniority used to protect a worker from lay offs, and every year at work contributed to a retirement package that was guaranteed after thirty years. The shutdown of a plant instantly shatters any hope of a secure future and the opportunity to bequeath a better life to one's children than they had. In *Diagnosing America,* Shepard Forman examines American exceptionalism in relation to the current demographic, economic, and social changes taking place in the United States. He concluded that the American Dream is in jeopardy because there is no longer a promise of material advance or social opportunities to improve one's class. Working a low wage service job offers little or no prospect of advancing within the organization without the proper educational credentials, which is impossible to pay for on such a low income.[31]

Since the nineteenth century, the heartland of the United States has been the Midwest. The industry of this heartland provided the armaments to win the Civil War, two world wars, and transformed America into a world superpower. The replacement of the region's manufacturing with foreign imports has wrought great suffering upon the displaced workers, their families, their communities, and the United States as a whole. The continued deindustrialization of America is destroying the middle class, widening the gap between the have and the have nots, and turning the "American Dream" into a nightmare.

The Auto-Industry and Decay in Cleveland

The Decline of the U.S. Auto-Industry

The late 1970s and early 1980s was an especially rough time for industrial workers of the American Midwest. Although the entire United States was affected by deindustrialization, this study focuses mainly on deindustrialization in Ohio because it was one of the states that suffered the most. Bennett Harrison, a Massachusetts Institute of Technology professor, demonstrated the severity of the region's economic devastation in a report to the Joint Economic Committee of Congress. Harrison showed that, between 1979 and 1984, the Midwest lost 1 million jobs that paid $28,000 or more on average, but only gained 900,000 jobs, which only paid a mere $7,500 a year or less. In Ohio, every 168 jobs lost to plant shutdowns were replaced by only 100 other jobs. Essentially, two out of every five displaced workers in Ohio could expect to find a job; however, most would be accepting a drastic pay cut.[32]

The plight of General Motors' Fisher Body Division demonstrates the severity of deindustrialization in Ohio. In 1921, Fisher Body Company opened its first Cleveland plant on Coit Road on the east side. By 1924, the facility employed 7,000 employees Then, in 1926, General Motors acquired the plant. After the pro-labor Wagner Act was passed during Franklin Delano Roosevelt's New Deal, General Motors recognized the United Auto Workers (UAW) union following a strike in December of 1936. Employment at the plant would hit its peak of 14,000 during World War II. Around the same time, in 1943, a plant in nearby Euclid was built to manufacture airplane parts; but, after the war, the plant was acquired by Fisher Body to also produce automobile bodies. Unfortunately, employment at the plants would steadily decline until the Coit Road plant and the Euclid plant, despite union concessions and maneuvers, closed down. The Coit Road plant shut down in 1983, and the Euclid plant finally closed its doors in 1993 after several reprieves and cutbacks. General Motors shifted some production in the Fisher Body plants to more modern plants in Michigan and increased its imports from foreign companies in partnership with General Motors.[33]

Throughout much of America's history, the construction of new plants used to be dictated by local energy costs, the proximity of raw materials, and market access. Technology, however, has changed that. Since the Industrial Revolution during the nineteenth century, advances in technology have cut communication and transportation costs so dramatically that goods may be manufactured almost anywhere, regardless of geographical concerns. This development has increased the importance of labor as a cost variable. Manufacturers have taken advantage of the advancements in technology to disinvest in older companies and industries in regions where unions have traditionally been strong, and they have been reinvesting in areas where they can dictate labor terms, such as in many southern states or overseas.[34]

In order to shift capital from one plant to another, a company usually opens a "parallel plant" in another location. These parallel plants make identical products and are created to leverage a company's dealings with unions and force them to make concessions. Since the New Deal, the Midwest states have maintained a strong union base. Many states in the Sunbelt have right-to-work laws, and state politicians have generally been against the development of strong unions; thus, many companies have built parallel plants in the Sunbelt rather than investing in their existing plants in the Midwest. Many local governments that are desperate to attract good manufacturing jobs offer generous incentive packages in an effort to outbid other cities. The promise of jobs and the multiplier effect that those jobs will have on the surrounding community often leads to millions of dollars in tax breaks and subsidies, which offer the company more incentives to move and build parallel plants.[35]

Since World War II, the automobile industry has become well known for shifting production to the American South or overseas and then closing down their plants in the Midwest. For example, in 1979, Goodyear Tires relocated a $180 million radial tire plant from Ohio to Oklahoma. Goodyear took six bids from six different jurisdictions and chose a location in Lawton, Oklahoma, which offered to move highways, build access roads to the highway, and to annex a school jurisdiction just so the manager's children could attend a good school.[36]

Similarly, when General Motors closed the Fisher Body plant on Coit Road, along with two other plants in Detroit, the company made demands on Detroit in exchange for a new modern GM plant to be built in the city. General Motors demanded Detroit to clear over four-hundred acres in an area known as Poletown for the construction of the Detroit-Hamtramck Assembly Plant. This clearing forced 3,200 people from their homes, destroyed 160 community businesses, relocated the on and off ramps for the city's expressways, and gave a 12-year tax abatement in return for a promise to build a plant there. All the construction and the relocation of the displaced residents was done with city tax dollars, which amounted to approximately $450 million. The plant was supposed to create 6,200 jobs, yet—as of 2014—the plant only employed roughly 1,600 employees.[37]

The practice of using parallel plants to force down labor costs and the blackmailing of cities to procure tax abatements and subsidization have been justified by the automobile industry as necessary in order to be competitive with foreign imports. The automobile industry and other manufacturing industries have been particularly vulnerable to foreign competition. In a study on "International Trade and Job Displacement in U.S. Manufacturing, 1979-1991," Lori G. Kletzer shows that "Almost every study of job displacement...has noted, at least in passing, the likely role of increased international competition in manufacturing job loss."[38] Kletzer's study demonstrates results that are "broadly consistent with the perception that imports displace some domestic jobs," and shows a "strong positive relationship between increases in import share and job displacement for industries long identified as import sensitive."[39]

The argument that American manufacturing is import sensitive should come as no surprise. Countries that are less developed than the United States have a comparative advantage in low and unskilled laborers because their labor costs are so low. Many proponents of free trade and globalization claim that the unions have inflated their wages and benefits to such an extreme that they are to blame for the uncompetitiveness of American manufacturing. Unions may have over-inflated their wages and utilized byzantine work rules that hamper efficiency, but the mistakes of the workers should not excuse the role that the United States government has played in opening up once protected American markets to foreign imports.

For two decades after World War II, businesses in the United States made record profits, and they easily entered into "social contracts" that entailed high wages and benefits for labor. When profit margins started eroding because of foreign competition, American manufacturers tried to cut costs mainly through reducing taxes and labor costs. The construction of parallel plants was an extremely powerful tool that was used by manufacturing companies to force concessions from unions and to solicit tax-abatements from local governments. Barry Bluestone describes parallel plants as part of a grander strategy based on capital mobility, which entails the shifting of capital from one corporate division to another, one industry to another, north to south, urban to rural, and relocating operations abroad. By pursuing this strategy of parallel plants and capital mobility, manufacturers could play workers in different areas or plants against one another and different cities against one another.[40]

The Case of Fisher Body

The Fisher Body division of General Motors fell victim to this strategy of capital mobility when the production at its plants was moved to other parts of the country and overseas. In February of 1982, GM announced it would be closing the Fisher Body plant on Coit Road. The devastating news came only a week after General Motors had announced that it would be closing the Fisher Body plant in Euclid. The Coit Road metal fabrication plant had 1,150 hourly and 380 salaried employees when GM announced the closing. Over one-thousand employees had already been recently laid off, and over a thousand more lost their job at the plant in Euclid.[41]

The loss of Coit Road entailed a loss of $1.5 million in direct tax revenue, and was a blow to local businesses and schools. Once the ripple effect passed through the hundreds of other businesses in the area that directly or indirectly conducted business with Fisher Body, the loss in tax revenues paid annually was estimated at $38.5 million. The shutdown did not merely displace a handful of industrial workers, but depressed an entire community. The helplessness and desperation the displaced workers and their communities felt can be witnessed in an opinion piece in *The Plain Dealer* by Elmer G. Chamberlain. Chamberlain demonstrated the rage of automobile workers from the plant by proclaiming that since the "administration, Congress, and GM don't give a damn for the American auto, steel or rubber workers, and other unemployed workers in related industries, we—the auto workers, steel and rubber workers—must do something, FAST!"[42] Chamberlain went on to call for boycotts and pickets of General Motors' car dealerships. These were futile suggestions, as the workers were virtually powerless to prevent the shutdown, and could only hope to placate General Motors enough to encourage them to reconsider.[43]

In response to the announcement that General Motors was planning to shut down the Fisher Body plants, state and local politicians and officials asked GM to reconsider. Immediately, the Ohio development director, James Duerk, planned to fly to Detroit to meet with GM officials. The initial consensus among policy makers was that General Motors was looking for a tax package, and the Mayor of Cleveland, George V. Voinovich, began discussing plans for a tax-free zone. Ohio governor, James A. Rhodes, even suggested passing new laws particularly tailored for General Motors. The tax breaks were being suggested as if they were a factor in General Motors' decision, but a Cleveland State University professor, Dr. John F. Burke Jr, pointed the blame on the shoulders of the entire automobile industry. Burke asserted that the auto industry needed to automate and cut jobs to survive, and that the auto workers and management were overpaid. He said, "It got out of line, too much out of line, and now its the day of reckoning." [44] However, the factor of foreign competition and the United States trade policy was not mentioned in Burke's critique.

Reacting to the shutdown announcements of the two Fisher Body plants, the auto workers accused General Motors of using threats of plant closings as "strong-arm tactics" to force the United

Auto Workers to the bargaining table. This claim was really not far from the truth, considering the threat of plant closure or the use of parallel plants in order to garner tax breaks and union concessions had been a common tactic used by the auto industry for years. The Coit Road plant manager, George P. Wiggins, cited GM data that estimated that other domestic suppliers could make the Fisher Body products for 50%, or $10 less an hour in total costs, than at the Coit Road plant. It is no wonder that the Union Local 45 had "an uneasy feeling among workers that the closing could be a ploy by GM to get the Union back to the table."[45] Michael Kelly in a *Cleveland Plain Dealer* article, "GM's strategy: Force UAW into concessions," voiced his belief that the threat of shutting down the Coit Road plant was a ploy by GM to get tax concessions from the local governments and contract concessions from the UAW. Kelly was sure that the company had spread rumors of the shut down for years, all while refusing to negotiate with the unions, and now GM wanted to talk on their own terms. The workers did not have much of a choice in the matter because they were beyond the age where they could reasonably expect to start over in a different career. The average age of the workers at the plant was 53 years old, and the average seniority was 30 years. It is extremely difficult for individuals nearing retirement to find any prospects for a new career.[46]

Underlying Structural Issues and Policy

Any concessions by unions may have served to correct the gap in productivity, but there existed an underlying structural policy that was discouraging investment in American productivity. Even though union pay and benefits were relatively high and did hamper competitiveness, the industrial worker cannot bear the sole burden of guilt. The manufacturing companies were complicit in granting concessions to unions in the decades following World War II; however, American industry could have held onto its competitive edge nonetheless. From 1950 to 1965 the United States had the highest productivity rate and the highest rate of federal government spending on research and development. After 1965, federal investment in research and development declined. Private capital investments also declined, thus relative productivity fell. Goods produced in the United States became more expensive than foreign imports because workers' wages rose faster than their productivity. The Department of Commerce estimated that if 1950's levels of investment would have continued, then each household would be earning $5,500 more than the 1982 median income of 18,800.[47]

In an attempt to save their jobs, the UAW voted for a pay freeze, trimmed $1.50 to $2.00 off their average hourly-rate of $19.80 an hour, and other concessions for job protections and profit-sharing. But General Motors did not wait for the vote to cancel all paid personal holidays two weeks before the vote was scheduled, which upset the union workers. Auto analyst, John H. Hammond, of Data Resources Inc. said that "GM workers aren't aware of the real bind the corporation is in financially and in terms of the long-term competitiveness of the product."[48] Japan's auto industry had become more efficient and productive than its counterpart in the United States in every way, and the concessions failed to fix the underlying structural problems that had caused this gap between the two countries. The give-backs would reduce the cost per car by $300 to $400, but it could not bridge the $1500 per car advantage that the Japanese manufacturers held.[49]

Despite the data that showcased the hopelessness of such small concessions, the GM workers approved the new contract. The auto workers at the Fisher Body plants conceded annual wage increases, paid personal holidays, and cost of living increases, but they failed to preserve their jobs permanently. The Coit Road plant received a two-year moratorium on the closing and a promise for 80% of the workers to be relocated to other plants; however, it would not be long until those promised relocation would be laid off indefinitely and find themselves as displaced workers. The Euclid plant was kept open by GM, but would eventually close shop ten years later in 1993.[50]

After two months of negotiations between the auto workers and General Motors, in May of 1982, it was announced that the Fisher Body plant at Coit Road would be phased out within 18 months. The UAW voted for concessions, which averaged $5 an hour per employee, but that was not enough for GM. The company estimated that it would save about $40 million a year from closing the Coit Road plant, but the city would lose $2 million in income tax. Mayor George V. Voinovich lamented the closing by remarking, "I think everyone did as much as they could to keep the plant open, I don't know what more they could have done."[51] A year later, Voinovich designated the day the plant closed, August 13, 1983, as Cleveland Coit Road Plant Commemoration Day.[52]

The shutting down of the Fisher Body plant was just one of many plants that GM shut down in the early 1980s. The company was shifting its manufacturing of subcompact cars from the United States to Japan, and planning to import them to the American market. GM, which already owned 34.2% of Isuzu Motors Ltd., was investing an additional $200 million to increase its shares in Isuzu Motors Ltd. to 40%. American suppliers to GM were giving a 2% discount to General Motors in order to help the company compete. These domestic suppliers railed about GM's history of investment overseas and decided to make a stand by canceling the company's discount in protest. It is unfortunate that a similar national protest did not take place long before companies like GM had invested so much money into foreign companies. This effort to force GM to reverse its outsourcing overseas would prove to be too little too late.[53]

By the 1980's, the United States trade policy had been encouraging Japanese and European imports for decades, and the effect of that policy was causing a decline in manufacturing across America. In response to the announcement that the Coit Road plant was closing in two to eighteen months, Charlie Wilkins, a committeeman at UAW Local 45 at the plant, said in disgust, "When it comes down to you and me, we're not the bottom line."[54] GM slashed domestic production and began buying small Japanese cars because it was cheaper to buy from overseas than to manufacture at home. But the reason it was cheaper to produce cars in Japan was a direct result of American trade policy towards Japan.

The United States encouraged American companies to invest in Japanese industry, and gave Japanese products access to the American market without requiring Japan to accept American products. In 1982, the year when General Motors announced the closing of the Fisher Body Coit Road plant, Japanese trade restrictions barred American trucks altogether and limited American cars to a mere 3,200 out of a market of 2,249,000. Japanese regulations, tariffs and other extra costs, such as requiring every import to be repainted in Japan, have been used by Japan to gain unfair trade advantages. By 1983, 50 to 70 percent of total profits for the largest three Japanese automobile companies were from sales in the United States. An outraged American citizen, James Tabatha, wrote in a *Cleveland Plain Dealer* opinion piece that "The bottom line is that Japan does not practice free trade. We are getting tired of Japan making excuses for her trade policies. We should retaliate by enacting taxes on Japanese cars and trucks and strictly limiting the number."[55] Yet American policy makers continued a trade policy that was detrimental to the United States' economy, and have since extended it to include countries like South Korea and China.[56]

The emerging competitive global environment demanded and still demands flexibility to move in any direction that may be required, and the best way to ensure flexibility for a company is to retain a high level of liquidity. This environment also has encouraged mergers. The merging and consolidation of companies has been an increasing trend ever since the nineteenth century. Companies have used consolidation in order to better safeguard their business from the perils of competition. Bluestone and Harrison say, "The ability to grow, diversify, shift gears, and purchase protection from nationalization by foreign governments, all require sufficient liquidity to be able to pay the bills. This constant need for cash explains why conglomerate managers are often quite prepared to sell even profitable subsidiaries."[57] Thus, as companies merge and consolidate into multinational companies, they lose their loyalty to the United States and seek profits with a complete disregard for what they are doing to the American nation or people. General Motors shut down the Fisher Body plants so that it could increase imports from Japanese manufacturers that they partially owned. A multinational corporation cares little for a handful of workers in Cleveland, Ohio, or any other American workers, despite the fact that American workers are relied on by these multinational corporations as their main consumers.[58]

A multinational corporation not only has no loyalty to the United States, but is also not subject to local pressures and could care less about some plant in a distant community. Moreover, when multinational corporations choose to close a plant, such a decision is usually related to overproduction. Thus, no matter what concessions they might receive, they remain uncommitted to keeping the plant open. In contrast, a local company usually faces bankruptcy and primarily wants to keep the plant open. Local companies are more willing to work with local governments, but multinational corporations make demands on local governments and play one city against another.[59]

Local politicians have the most vested interest in preventing plant closings but have little control and not much to offer without assistance from the state or federal governments because local governments are the weakest. Public policy is a collective endeavor of national, state, and local governments, but they are not always in agreement when it comes to what policies to pursue. Some local governments take a passive role by deferring to the private sector and solely work to provide a framework for unions and the company to work out an agreement in regards to the plant, but this inactivity is rare. A more active role involves the offering of key economic resources, such as financial assistance packages or retaining centers for workers. The city of Cleveland attempted to play a more active role in preventing the closing of the Fisher Body plants, but the city did not offer much more than tax abatements. Likewise, when GM closed two plants in Detroit, the city, not only granted tax abatements, but also subsidized the construction of a new plant in Poletown and used eminent domain to evict residents and businesses.

Detroit did everything it could short of implementing anti-plant-closing laws or filing lawsuits against General Motors.[60]

In most cases, the local government is helpless to prevent plant closings without assistance from higher levels of government. Addressing each specific incident with such ineffective local laws or lawsuits is akin to combating a disease by merely addressing the symptoms. Rather than dealing with deindustrialization on a case by case basis, the United States needs to alter the underlying root causes of deindustrialization. A more thorough reassessment of the United States' trade policy and tax codes could address the dysfunctional structural problems that have caused deindustrialization and the driving of investment overseas. Neither the city government in Cleveland nor the state government of Ohio could do anything to prevent General Motors from closing the Fisher Body plants. Only a top down approach towards industry at the national level could have helped the auto workers of Cleveland.

The Decline of Steel in the Mahoning Valley

History of Republic Steel

In 1899, Republic Iron & Steel Company was founded in Youngstown, Ohio. Three decades later on April 8, 1930, Republic Iron and Steel Company, along with an amalgamation of many other smaller iron and steel companies in Youngstown, reorganized into Republic Steel. Throughout the 1930s, Republic Steel continued to grow both locally and nationally. In 1935, Truscon Steel Company in Youngstown was acquired. In 1936, Corrigan McKinney Steel Company in Cleveland, Ohio was acquired. And in 1937, Gulf States Steel in Gadsden, Alabama was acquired. Thus, Republic Steel became the third largest steel company in the United States, after U.S. Steel and Bethlehem Steel, and helped to make the Mahoning Valley into the center of steel production.[61]

During that same time, Republic Steel and other Steel companies resisted efforts by its employees to unionize. The "little steel" strike of 1937 erupted among the workers of Republic Steel, Youngstown Sheet & Tube, and Inland Steel. The strike eventually came to an end when the Ohio governor, Martin Davey, called in the Ohio National Guard to deal with the strikers. Five years later, on August 11, 1942, the company relented and signed its first contract with the United Steelworkers of America. This agreement was made possible because of the environment surrounding World War II, when the company was running at full capacity and was still making generous profits despite price controls. In this climate, the company could make concessions to the workers, modernize its facilities, and still make a profit at the same time.[62]

After the war, strikes occurred throughout the 40's and 50's and led to gradual increases in wages, but undermined the reliability of the steel industry. In 1952, President Truman attempted to seize steel plants in order to ward off an impending strike that could have jeopardized steel production during the Korean War. This seizure of Youngstown Sheet and Tube was challenged, and the Supreme Court ruled the seizure illegal and returned the plant to the company. Later that decade, a strike that began on July 15, 1959 and lasted 116 days led to a shortage and the importing of foreign steel. Paul Gerhardt, an associate professor of industrial relations at Case Western Reserve University, said in 1986 that the 116-day strike in 1959 was so devastating for both the companies and the unions that there was a tacit agreement that workers would not strike in return for rising wages and benefits between 1959 and 1986. Also, because of the length of the 1959 strike, it allowed foreign competition—for the first time—to make large inroads into the American economy. Gerhardt said that "It was a turning point in the steel industry. Companies began saying that they didn't want to bother with American steel companies because they were always striking, so they took their business abroad."[63] Foreign imports would continue to be an ever-increasing problem beyond 1986 up to, and including, today.[64]

In the decades following the 1959 strike, the economic situation of Republic Steel worsened until it became precarious. Facility improvements continued through the 1960s, but by the end of the 1960s environmental controls became a costly issue. The 1970s witnessed further economic difficulties for steel and other manufacturing industries due to inflation, foreign imports, environmental control costs, and price controls. Republic Steel become unsustainable in the early 1980s, and on March 21, 1984, Republic Steel merged with Jones and Laughlin Steel to create LTV Steel Company in order to reduce overhead costs. LTV was not originally a steel company, but became a steel company through mergers and acquisitions, such as the merger with Republic in 1984. It was founded in 1947 by James Ling as a Dallas based electronics company. In 1960 Ling acquired Temco, a missile company, and the following year acquired Chance Vought, a fighter plane manufacturer, which created Ling-Temco-Vought (LTV). LTV originally entered the steel business in 1968 by acquiring Jones & Laughlin Steel Corp. In 1978, the conglomerate acquired Youngstown Sheet and Tube before merging with Republic Steel. On July 17, 1986, LTV filed for Chapter 11 bankruptcy. LTV was hoping to reorganize itself and possibly escape liability for $2.3 billion in unfunded pension funds.[65]

On December 2 1986, in response to news of possible pension cuts, hundreds of retired and idled steelworkers protested in front of the LTV headquarters. The pension fund was depleted by lump sum payments that were offered as a way to buy-out worker's pensions, but it left those who wanted to hold on to their pensions the prospect that they could lose everything. In addition to the unfunded pension liabilities, LTV was seeking protection from over 20,000 creditors of banks, companies, and firms, and it owed $130 million in bonds that were issued with the Ohio state seal in order to pay for pollution controls.[66]

The bankruptcy reorganization took place through the selling off of multiple facilities and multiple indefinite idlings of facilities, which reduced steel production capacity from twenty-four-million tons to ten-million tons per year. A federal agency, the Pension Benefit Guarantee Corporation (PBGC) had assumed three of LTV's pension plans but tried to transfer them back to LTV, which LTV tried to block, but lost in the Supreme Court. LTV then sold its high tech industries of aerospace and defense in an attempt to pay for a portion of the $2.3 billion of pension promises.[67]

David H Hoag, who took over as CEO from Raymond A. Hay during the bankruptcy, had 30 years of experience in the steel business. Hoag's chapter eleven plan was to make LTV a viable company again by focusing primarily on its steel assets. He cut the defense company's portfolio and focused on working out a deal to take care of the $2.3 billion of unfunded pensions that were returned to LTV from PBGC by the Supreme Court. Because of his efforts, Hoag has been credited with leading the reorganization of LTV and creating a strong base of high-quality and cost-efficient facilities. On June 28, 1993, LTV came out of bankruptcy reorganized into two main divisions: LTV Steel and LTV Energy Products. Two years later, LTV Energy Products was sold, making LTV primarily a steel company. And during the late 1990's and early 2000's, LTV set out to expand its steel production by purchasing Copperweld Corporation and Copperweld Canada, but it also sold off assets in Presque Isle Corporation and shutdown operations in LTV Steel Mining in January of 2000 because they were no longer profitable.[68]

Unfortunately, due to low steel prices, competition from foreign imports, and a weakening U.S. economy, LTV declared bankruptcy for a second time on December 29, 2000. The "bridge to the future," a 5 year restructuring plan, was introduced in April 2001 in order to make LTV a viable company again. LTV sold off more of its assets, received tax breaks and discounted rates, but the company could not broker a deal with the union and could no longer remain in business. W. L. Ross and Company purchased LTV's steel assets but avoided pension costs because they did not buy LTV Corporation. Thus, the pensions were picked up by the government. The sale also gave a federal abatement of pollution rules and subsidies. LTV Steel's assets were incorporated into the International Steel Group, which merged with Mittal Steel USA to form the largest steel company in the world.[69]

Investments, Capital, and the Issue with Labor

There were multiple reasons why LTV and much of the steel industry succumbed to foreign competition. The high wages and benefits garnered by unions greatly exaggerated labor costs compared to foreign companies. The added costs of complying with environmental regulations were also a huge drain on the economic resources of domestic manufacturers; however, the fact of the matter is that American companies created their own competition. American companies offered companies in Germany and Japan technology in exchange for royalties. These joint production arrangements used investments from American companies to create plants overseas that would be turned over to the host nation; thus creating their own future competition that would undermine American industry.[70]

The siphoning of funds overseas led to a lack of investment in domestic industries. A main reason for deindustrialization in America was the inability for companies like Youngstown Sheet and Tube to maintain the modernization of their plants because the money was being invested overseas. Youngstown Sheet and Tube Company's parent company, Lyke Corporation, was unable to acquire the funds to modernize its plants because its three principal bankers began denying it loans in the mid-1970's. At the same time, these banks shifted investments to the Japanese steel industry. For example, between 1975 and 1977, Citibank increased loans to Japanese steel companies from $59 million to over $230 million,

Chase Manhattan increased its investments in Japanese steel companies from $59 million to over $204 million, and the Chemical Bank of New York's loans to Japanese steel companies rose from $15 million to over $82 million. Ironically, U.S. Steel Corporation led the domestic steel industry in protesting foreign steel, which they claimed was flooding the U.S. market with cheap steel. However, U.S. Steel was just one company that, while complaining domestically about foreign steel imports, was also investing abroad in that very same competition instead of investing in its domestic companies for upgrades. The 1979 Annual Report for U.S. Steel listed partial ownership of eleven foreign companies that were competing with its domestic holdings.[71]

Since the rate of return on investments overseas was higher, American conglomerates began using domestic subsidiaries as "cash cows" for money to invest overseas. These were mature companies with a high market share, but with low potential growth rates. Once acquired by conglomerates, their profits were used for investment overseas in companies with low market shares and high potential growth rates. It was more profitable to invest overseas than to invest domestically because foreign companies often had and continue to have more potential for growth. This increased potential naturally translates into a higher rate of return on investment. It was also cheaper to use profits from a subsidiary instead of taking out loans to invest overseas. As a domestic subsidiary was continuously milked, eventually it would not be able to meet the rate of return (even if they were still turning a profit) set by their parent corporation to provide enough money for investment overseas. When this scenario occurred, the facilities generally were sold off or shut down so that their assets could be liquefied and invested overseas in what equaled a higher rate of return for the parent corporation. For example, in 1969 Youngstown Sheet and Tube Company was purchased by Lykes Corporation out of New Orleans. Following the purchase, Lykes used the profits of Youngstown Sheet and Tube Company to pay off the debt incurred from the purchase and to invest overseas. Lykes had purposefully undertook a planned disinvestment in Youngstown Sheet and Tube in order to invest the profits of the plant elsewhere. Thus, the deindustrialization of Youngstown began as greed and the desire to maximize profits no matter what the cost to workers, communities, or the nation.[72]

Environmental Regulations and Their Costs

Environmental codes and regulations regarding pollution have long been cited as playing a major role in the uncompetitiveness of United States industries, a major factor in large-scale deindustrialization. Those in favor of environmental regulations usually rationalize the costs of implementing such policies and downplay their effects on the competitiveness of American industry. Those opposed to environmental regulations usually cite them as a factor of the unfriendly business environment in America that has brought about deindustrialization. The truth is that there are multiple factors that have contributed to deindustrialization; therefore it is easy for any one individual to disregard several factors and focus on the factors that most readily assimilate into their world epistemology. While environmental regulations and the costs of pollution controls that go along with such regulations have contributed to the failings of American industry, they are not solely responsible. It is possible to implement environmental regulations without directly hampering a business's competitiveness; however, to plot a new course, one must learn from the mistakes of the past.

One such mistake occurred in 1977 in Youngstown. Republic Steel had failed to implement certain pollution controls mandated on its holdings in the Mahoning Valley facilities in Ohio. Republic Steel believed many of the new regulations were too expensive, and they did not agree with the Environmental Protection Agency's methodology. The EPA was determined to force immediate action on Republic Steel, and the appeal filed by Republic Steel read as follows:

> In view of the tremendous impact which the plan will have on Republic, it is entitled to no less...Republic retained ADL (Arthur D. Little, Inc. consulting firm) to prepare comments and to develop, using the EPA methodology, alternative control strategies that would attain and maintain the ambient air quality standards for SO2 but in a less costly manner...The proposal took EPA a year to develop and employed complex new computer modeling techniques, but EPA granted only 74 days for public comment...It is the view of Republic that respondents' motion (to consider filings) represents the latest in a series of attempts by EPA to insulate the Ohio sulfur dioxide implementation plan from adequate public comment and judicial review.[73]

Republic petitioned for extensions, but the EPA claimed Republic Steel deliberately delayed implementation; however, Republic Steel claimed that the EPA was responsible for the delay. The court proceedings would follow a similar back and forth pattern.

After the EPA standards were forced on Republic Steel, the standards would continue to be readjusted and fixed at tighter and tighter levels by the EPA. For example; in order to meet EPA standards, Youngstown Sheet and Tube apportioned $31 million in an anti-pollution program to reduce and treat pollutants in the Mahoning River on October 30, 1973. An additional $5 million was financed by the state through the Ohio Water Development Authority. Yet more restrictions and pollution requirements were issued by the EPA just a few short years later in 1977. Water pollution control equipment upgrades would now cost $48.5 million. Air pollution abatement equipment upgrades would cost $53.4 million. Solid waste control equipment upgrades would cost $13.6 million. These figures also failed to account for the cost of sulfur dioxide (SO2) controls.[74]

In the Mahoning Valley, Republic Steel had six facilities that generated a net cash flow of $24 million under the most optimistic performance predictions, but less than $1 million under the average performance predictions. Both estimates were negative after adding pollution control costs, which would have created a 15 year cumulative deficit of between $14 million and $372 million in the average case scenario and a 15 year cumulative cash flow of $92 million in the best case scenario. After taking into account the pollution control costs, it would have been hard to imagine the plants being operated on a profitable basis. These figures show that there was no rational reason for Republic Steel to implement the pollution controls. Because of this reality the courts granted Republic Steel a status as a special "subcategory" for Mahoning Valley. This categorization froze the pollution standards at the then current discharge levels because of the company's unique economic disadvantage and the effects the loss of the plants would have on the socioeconomic factors of the greater community. Unfortunately, this ruling was later overturned. The Federal courts invalidated the EPA exemptions, which meant that Republic Steel would have to invest in the pollution controls that it could ill afford.[75]

Environmental regulations and pollution controls definitely adversely affected the profitability of companies; however, without foreign competition and capital flight overseas, the costs of controls could have been weathered more easily. The government also assumed a small percentage of pollution costs by issuing government bonds. Since the EPA mandated and was enforcing these regulations as a government agency, it only seems reasonable that the government should have developed a method of paying for a larger portion or even the majority of such pollution controls instead of placing the bulk of the costs on the industry itself. If a company is forced out of business because it cannot afford to implement arbitrary pollution controls, then nobody wins. The loss of tax bases and an increase in government expenditures associated with plant closings far outweighs the costs of assisting industry in financing pollution control upgrades. The damages caused to displaced workers of closed down plants far surpasses any damage undone by environmental regulations. In regards to the EPA regulations, a Youngstown area mayor, Nick J. Eramo of Girard, said that, "When you see smoke, people are working - no smoke, something's wrong.

I'm all for clean air, but my dad lived to be 75. He ate all that dirt. He didn't die of pollution. He had a heart attack. They want to clean our river, but what are people going to do, fish for a living?"[76]

[illegible]

Loss of Identity, Health Issues, and Depopulation

On September 19, 1977, the Youngstown Sheet and Tube Company announced the closing of the Campbell Works. Five-thousand jobs were lost within a few months, and a further fifty-thousand steel workers would lose their jobs within the next five years. Unemployment in the Youngstown area would rise to over twenty-percent and would not fall below double-digits for the next decade. Deindustrialization in Youngstown entailed the loss of status and self-esteem. The steel mills defined Youngstown, and the steelworkers viewed themselves as contemporary cowboys whose jobs were very physical, and they disdained white collar workers who took three-hour lunches with their clients. Displaced industrial workers lost more than their jobs. They lost their pride that was based on a job that required hard work and physical prowess. The service jobs that replaced the steel mill jobs were based on educational credentials and were traditionally female jobs. The loss of a steel job in Youngstown entailed the loss of one's pride and manhood. [77]

Bruce Springsteen's song "Youngstown" glorifies steelworkers and laments the effects the demise of the steel industry has had on Youngstown. The lyrics tell how his daddy came home from World War II to work the steel mills and how he came home from Vietnam to do the same. He also emphasizes the steel mill's importance to national security with the lyrics that "these mills they built the tanks and guns that won this country's wars."[78] He also makes it clear in the song that those same steel mills were not just the lifeblood of the city, but the literal provider for the worker's families, without which they would starve.[79]

Conservatives blamed deindustrialization on regulations and used it to promote deregulation. They also cited creative destruction, the idea that bad investments need to be allowed to fail in order to open up capital for newer and more efficient avenues of economic development. They even went as far to blame the individual for being lazy or the union for being entitled. Liberals blamed corporate greed and claimed that Youngstown had been "downsized" or victimized by corporations. Both had touched upon parts of the equation. Corporate greed has influenced plant relocation abroad, which reflects the company's desire for a controllable workforce that is inexpensive and compliant. At the same time, plant relocations have also been a company's response to an increasing sense of entitlement and militancy among union workers. However, deindustrialization in Youngstown and across the nation has been far more complicated than the simple blaming of either capitalists or labor. That is an old dichotomy that fails to take in the overarching structural problems in the American economy and the American government that have led the country down this path.[80]

In 2009, Sean Safford compared the post-deindustrialization recovery of Allentown, Pennsylvania with Youngstown due to their similarities in industrial concentration and deindustrialization. Allentown made a recovery and continues to be a globally competitive industrial city, whereas Youngstown's recovery has been significantly less successful. Safford attributes the discrepancy in recoveries to the ability of Allentown to bring together and nurture social networks through community institutions. The displaced workers of Youngstown lost their social networks with their jobs, and the lack of social networks made it difficult for the local economy to rally its recovery. He argues that a community needs a multiplicity of of networks, such as sport teams, religious establishments, and recreational clubs that can tie people together and offer avenues of information and opportunities.[81]

In a ten year period beginning in 1977, a succession of shutdowns resulted in the loss of over 50,000 jobs in the steel and related industries in Youngstown. Effects of the shutdowns lingered for decades. Youngstown lost half its population, families were disintegrated, and nonviolent crimes and domestic violence rose. Fifteen years after the initial closings, homicides and gang violence associated with the dealing of drugs and protecting gang territory increased as the children of broken homes and communities came of age with little or no opportunities. Twenty-five years later, the area held high levels of "unemployment, poverty rates, population decline, devaluation of housing stock, foreclosures, bankruptcies, and arsons."[82] The county Youngstown is located in went from a normal rate of crime and homicides to one of the top 10 in the nation. [83]

Richard B. McKenzie believes it is the responsibility of the unions to get closing notifications and to work out severance contracts. He states in *Plant Closings* that, "Restrictions on business closings will, in the long run especially, lead to greater costs of production, higher prices on consumer goods, and lower real incomes—and not only in the region in which they are imposed: They are, in the long run, necessarily detrimental to all regions."[84] He also says that layoffs and unemployment from plant closings are over exaggerated. This is because he believes that many plants relocate to the same region, new businesses migrate in, and that non-industrial job creation will take place. He claims that plant closings and relocation are only very small parts of the economic equation. He asserts that the average worker is not adversely affected by plant closings and anti-plant closing legislation would have unforeseen and devastating effects to the average worker. He also contends that unemployment from plant closings is insignificant.[85]

Thus far, this study has tended to show just the opposite. McKenzie's mistake is that he holds free enterprise and free-market capitalism up as an ideal, and he also smears any legislation to prevent plant-closings as an attack on capitalism. His entire approach is completely ideological in nature. Thus, the problem with McKenzie's analysis is that he fails to recognize that the United States has never truly operated under laissez-faire capitalism. America has always utilized the government to influence economic conditions and outcomes. Tariffs and trade barriers, monetary and fiscal policies, wealth redistribution programs, tax incentives and write-offs, bailouts, price controls, union legislation, and anti-trust suits have all played significant roles throughout American history. But the biggest mistake of McKenzie is his assumption that free-trade is, not only desirable, but also a moral practice. America has never operated under the auspices of free trade. In the early days of American independence, the federal government used tariffs to generate income. The Tariff Act of 1816 mandated the first universal tariff that taxed manufactured goods at 20 to 25 percent and raw materials at 15 to 20 percent. In total, thirteen tariff acts were passed between the American Revolution and World War II. Since then, the United States trade policy has been modified to encourage imports and discourage exports. This fact reveals the existence of real structural problems that have caused deindustrialization across the United States. There is no such thing as free trade in American trade policy, and there never has been.[86]

The demise of the steel industry and the plight of the Mahoning Valley serve as warning signs for the rest of America. The inflated wages and inefficient work rules of unions and the cost of pollution controls greatly inhibited the industry's ability to compete with foreign imports. The shifting of investments abroad not only prevented domestic companies from modernizing, but created the competition that would later threaten domestic steel producers. The desire to maximize profits led conglomerates to scrap domestic plants in favor of lucrative investment opportunities in foreign producers. And this all led to the deindustrialization of the Mahoning

Valley, which witnessed massive unemployment, depopulation, an explosion in crime, and suffering from health and mental complications. This is, not just the history of Youngstown, but also the future of America as a whole if deindustrialization continues.

Globalization, Trade and Industrial Policy

The Myth of Free Trade in America

The years 1680 to 1815 marked the historic period known as the Enlightenment. This period was defined by a philosophy of scientific inquiry, public debate, and democratic ideas that led to radical changes in societal and governmental institutions. America was founded during the Enlightenment, and its ideas have left their mark on the American political landscape. However, America was not founded as a capitalist paradise for robber barons as some conservative pundits claim. Throughout most of America's history it was understood by both private businesses and government officials that protective tariffs and barriers to international trade were not just beneficial, but necessary for the prosperity of domestic industries and for national economic strength. In 1944, during World War II, policy makers from America and Great Britain met at Bretton Woods, New Hampshire, and reversed their protectionist policies and agreed to universal rules on international economic activity. Since Bretton Woods there has been an increasing push towards "free trade" in America. Free trade has become part of the neoliberal rhetoric that perpetuates an agenda of globalization, including the pursuit of the breaking down of tariffs and trade barriers that supposedly hamper international trade and prosperity. But globalization and free trade do not unilaterally benefit the entire American nation. There are clear cut winners and losers in globalization. The winners have been international financiers and multinational corporations. The losers have been the American worker, both skilled and unskilled, and the American manufacturing industry as a whole.[87]

America is capital abundant because it has large amounts of capital relative to other nations; therefore, America has a comparative advantage in the global market in capital. Less developed nations have a comparative advantage in labor because as a whole they are labor abundant compared to the United States. Developing nations can also provide labor cheaper because of their lower cost of living and their willingness to work for less; thus, free trade benefits U.S. capital but harms U.S. labor. The neoliberal proponents of trade liberalization argue that free trade expands America's export market and will create more jobs than it destroys. Yet, America has not seen a huge upswing in exports. Opponents of trade liberalization point out that countries with lower labor costs and less regulations will outcompete domestic manufacturers and that domestic workers will in turn be hurt by unemployment, costly retraining, and lower wages.[88]

The liberalization of U.S. trade has created stiff competition for American workers because the developing world is abundant in unskilled workers; however, since the U.S. has high productivity and is technologically advanced, tech workers have traditionally fared fairly well. This disparity between tech and non-tech workers has contributed to the widening gap between the rich and the poor and created different rates of unemployment for each respective group. In a study, Jeffrey D. Sachs and Howard J. Shatz have concluded that "increased trade with low-wage countries will increase the wage inequality between high-skilled and low-skilled workers" in America. However, the issuing of H-1B visas has steadily been on the rise over recent decades. Instead of outsourcing tech jobs, America has been importing cheap tech workers to displace American tech workers. No American worker is safe from displacement caused by globalization.[89]

Advocates of free trade believe that "trade is good because the induced reallocation of a fixed amount of resources yields greater output....Artificial impediments to trade are bad because they prevent the most efficient allocation of the fixed amount of resources."[90] But free trade proponents offer no solutions that help to alleviate the problems facing those displaced from their "efficient allocation" of resources, nor do they put into perspective how this rearranging of society benefits or harms the national security and industrial strength of America as a whole. At best they may propose temporary programs that are meant to ease the troubles of displaced workers through training subsidies and unemployment insurance. Blind adherence to certain economic doctrines and models rely on assumptions that involve a perfect world of mere individuals and fails to take into account the needs and security of a nation as a whole. The reality is that America has never operated under mutually beneficial free trade as proponents would have one believe.[91]

America Opens its Markets to its Allies

The roots of advocacy for free trade in America began in the aftermath of World War II, during the incipient Cold War. Because America feared bad economic conditions would serve as a breeding ground for communism, a grant was offered to rebuild the European economy. The Marshall Plan issued $13 billion to rebuild Europe's industries and ensured the continent could export in order to drive its economy. In addition, American companies were given tax incentives by the government to transfer technology to foreign corporations in allied countries. But due to trade barriers, tariffs, and the poor economic state of America's allies, who had been greatly depressed during the war, there was a need to find a market to ensure the economic success of the non-communist world. There was a fear that America's allies would turn communist and switch sides to the Soviet bloc if their economic conditions were not improved. The goal of the Marshall Plan was to remake Western Europe into a second United States by integrating its economies in much the same way that the markets of the states in America were integrated. The purpose of such integration was to create a prosperous and stable Europe that was secure against communist influences, and create a Europe which could aid the United States in a new integrated world trade system. In 1953, the National Security Council stated that "economic deterioration and falling living standards...create fertile ground for communist subversion."[92] American officials determined that geopolitical concerns took precedence over domestic economic concerns; thus, they used access to the American market as a tool to cement Cold War alliances. The general consensus among American policymakers was that the sheer size and strength of American industry was so great that allowing Japan and Europe free access to the American market would cause little or no harm. However, granting allies access to the American market was not free trade because America's allies did not reciprocate by granting American companies access to their markets.[93]

In 1947, America entered into "free trade" with its Cold War allies through GATT (General Agreement on Tariffs and Trade), but none of America's allies practiced free trade. In Japan and Germany, the state subsidized its manufacturing industries and encouraged profits to be used as reinvestments in the industry instead of paying dividends to stockholders. Historian Judith Stein points out that "The United States looked the other way as Europe and Japan protected markets and discriminated against American producers...the large American market became the safety valve for the export industries of U.S. allies, who quickly became economic competitors."[94] This is not free trade, but protectionism inverted. Instead of protecting domestic industries from foreign competition and working to focus on increasing exports, the United States was seeking to increase imports while acquiescing to barriers against its own exports at the expense of its own industry, its own people, and its own national prosperity.[95]

The American government may not have worried much about the impediments placed on its own exports; however, domestic businesses did, and they would eventually find a way to penetrate the markets of America's trade partners. The solution was for American businesses to build plants overseas or to invest in a foreign business. For example, because of foreign trade barriers like the EEC (European Economic Community) American companies needed to manufacture in Europe if they wanted to sell in Europe. Some companies, like the heavy equipment manufacturer, Caterpillar, began building its parts overseas completely because they could then sell overseas and get past tariffs. Furthermore, they could still sell to the U.S. because of America's liberal trade policies, which did not tax imports. American corporate investment overseas robbed domestic plants of capital that was necessary to stay modernized and maintain competitive productivity levels.

Another example can be witnessed in the case of RCA. Throughout the 1970's, RCA bought other companies and invested overseas in a quest for cheap labor. The company could have invested in its productive capabilities so that it could have competed better with imports through automation and technological innovation. Unfortunately, the company had decided to deal with imports by moving its production abroad, which would inevitably lead to the shutdown of its domestic production in the United States.[96]

As the Cold War dragged on, the situation continued only to worsen. At every turn, strategic foreign policy concerns trumped economics. At the Kennedy Round trade negotiations in Geneva from May 1964 to June 1967, the United States continued to lower and strip American import quotas and tariffs, but received no reciprocal concessions from its allies. As a result, imports from Japan increased 96 percent between 1967 and 1970. Matters got even worse in January of 1974. The United States removed all restrictions on foreign investment, which immediately led to corporate capital shifts from domestic companies to foreign ones. This development further starved American companies of much needed investments and further hurt domestic productivity improvements. Accepting foreign imports eroded the market share and hurt the sales of domestic producers, but investing in foreign companies instead of domestic ones sentenced America's industry to death. If a company cannot stay modernized or increase productivity, then it will become uncompetitive and be destined to shut down in the near future. Conservatives, like Federal Reserve Chairman, Alan Greenspan, argued that the problem causing deindustrialization was "overconsumption, inflationary finance, deficit spending, excessive regulation, and a tax code hostile to capital formation."[97] However, the problem was not regulations or tax codes that prevented capital formation, but regulations and tax codes that encouraged capital to move overseas. This internationalization of trade that has been pursued by America has included the liberalization of financial institutions. The deregulation of interest rates and the removal of credit controls have led to the explosive growth of the investment banking business, but this development has not led to the investment of capital in American manufacturing. Investment has been drawn to certain hedge funds that buy and sell currencies and securities that speculate on profits from future production overseas. It is nothing more than speculating on speculation and it creates nothing of value —just speculative bubbles that burst. A perfect example is the Modernization Act of 1999, which removed legal divisions between investment and commercial banking, as well as divisions between insurance companies and brokerage houses. It was these deregulations that paved the way for the Great Recession and led to the bank bailout of 2009.[98]

Even during the recession of the mid 1970s American policy makers worried more about the economic well-being of America's Cold War allies than America's own economic well-being. The international recession of 1975 led the United States to accept the exports of allies who were suffering economically and to offer a fiscal package to encourage the purchasing of these exports by Americans in order to stimulate recovery. Behavior of this manner and continued poor tax codes and regulations led to the vast deindustrialization throughout America that was witnessed from the latter half of the 1970s into the 1990s. Neoliberal reforms in the tax code and deregulation of the financial sector fueled mergers, acquisitions, and buyouts. Underperforming companies that held valuable assets became the targets of hostile corporate takeovers that led to the selling off of those assets for windfall profits. Speculators and stockholders benefited from such predatory takeovers, but the average American suffered. [99]

In the 1990s, the United States began using low interest rates not just to stimulate the economies of its allies, but to stabilize the global economy and to buffer its allies from a possible economic downturn. During the late 1990's, the four Asian Tigers (Taiwan, South Korea, Singapore, and Hong Kong) had entered into an economic crisis. The economies of the Asian Tigers were dependent upon exports to the United States, and yet it was investments from America that helped to create these export industries in the first place. Continued investment created a speculative bubble that burst in the late 1990's, and the only way to stimulate a recovery was for the Tigers to increase exports. Since America was the main market for the Asian Tigers' exports, the Federal Reserve lowered interest rates to encourage Americans to borrow in order to purchase the Tigers' exports. Instead of using a fiscal stimulus as in the 1970s, a monetary stimulus was pursued with the Federal Reserve acting as the world's bank. This strategy has led to an American dependence on cheap credit from East Asia and Europe, but East Asia and Europe have also come to depend on the American consumers to purchase their goods. Export heavy countries, like the Asian Tigers, have high savings rates and loan that money to American borrowers so they can buy their exports. In essence, Americans buy the exports of East Asia and Europe on credit from those very same countries, who are willing to lend because their economies depend on exports to America. In 2005, Paul Krugman wrote "These days Americans make a living by selling each other houses, paid with money borrowed from China."[100]

The transformation of America into a nation that does not build anything of value, but only consumes products made around the globe, does not bode well for the nation's economic future. America's future is looking less and less like some idealized post-industrial utopia, but is looking more and more like a banana republic. For example, the top Japanese exports in 1984 to America consisted of motor vehicles, iron and steel plates, truck and tractor chassis, radios, motorcycles and motorbikes; whereas, the top U.S. exports to Japan consisted of soybeans, corn, fir logs, hemlock logs, coal, wheat, and cotton. However, the American finance sector seems to be doing very well from these developments.[101]

The Problem with Finance

A Wall Street investment banker, James Balog said, "We wouldn't run our families the way we run the economy... Corporations plan and the government should, too. Planning could help us look beyond the next election."[102] Any reference in America today involving "planning" is considered socialism. This way of thinking is owed to the American tradition of capitalism, but the United States has always been a mixed economy. There has never existed complete laissez-faire capitalism in the United States. The rhetoric against any type of planning has been whipped up by multinational corporations and financial institutions that benefit from these policies at the expense of the rest of America. There is no free trade in America's trade policy. Free trade in America is an ideal, a myth, and a fantasy. Capital has moved abroad because the tax code and tariff barriers to American exports encourage it to, but simple capital controls and tax policy would be able to keep capital at home and create jobs domestically.[103]

The steps to curtail the fleeing of capital overseas and to protect domestic industry from foreign imports have not been pursued because politicians and their campaign donors benefit from the current arrangement. Politics has trumped economics in American trade negotiations, and they seem poised to continue in this manner for the foreseeable future because individual politicians will only support deals that involve industries important to their constituencies, like beef and grapefruit, instead of tackling the structural policy problems. But to see who is perpetuating this system, one only needs to look at who benefits from this system. There is no doubt that no one benefits more from the economic and political trends more than the finance sector.[104]

The financial sector has benefited the most from deindustrialization because they are the ones who have invested overseas and who are now receiving those profits. They then use their profits to fund the campaigns of both Republicans and Democrats to ensure that the same policies continue uninterrupted. Since the 1970s, the financial sector in America has come to dominate the economy through deregulation, free trade, and tax policies that favor finance—which allowed them to create the crisis of 2008 with risky credit default swaps and other risky financial instruments. Yet in return, the financial institutions that caused the Great Recession were rewarded with a cash payout that was billed to the American taxpayers. The bailouts during the global financial crisis enabled financial conglomerates to continue losing more money without being forced to declare bankruptcy, and future generations of Americans will be forced to pay back the trillions of dollars that were used in the bailout. Barack Obama was elected on hope and change, but Obama's policies towards industry have not addressed the overarching structural problems facing American manufacturing, and business as usual since the 1970s has resumed for the financial sector.[105]

American capitalists have blamed deindustrialization on "high wages, high taxes, aging manufacturing plants, inflation, and the declining infrastructure of the American manufacturing heartland."[106] Yet, there is no mention of finance's role in shifting domestic investment overseas, which caused the manufacturing plants to age relative to the competition. And the financial sector has not just played a prominent role in shifting manufacturing overseas, but has also profited greatly in this process. While middle America is being forced into low-paying service jobs, the financial sector has been claiming higher and higher profits for themselves. This transition to a post-industrial society has greatly widened the gap between the rich and the poor. Between 1980 and 1988 alone, the number of millionaires doubled and the income share of the top 1% rose from 9% to 11%. Meanwhile, during the 1980s, domestic investments in new plants and machinery reached its lowest level since World War II. This discrepancy is a result of the fact that the millions being made have come almost wholly from investments in new plants and machinery overseas. Domestically, the rich have made their money through debt investment instead of capital investments. Money has been made through the buying and merging of domestic companies and liquefying the assets of those companies, and then moving the liquefied company's production overseas. This trend continues and means that ever increasing debt needs to be paid off with less and less available capital.[107]

As domestic capital dries up and debt is becoming an increasing burden in the private sector, public debt has also been increasing, and people are paying more and more taxes on less and less real income. In 1980, the United States was the largest creditor nation and had a trade surplus of $166 billion, but by 1987 the United States was the largest debtor nation and had a trade deficit of $166 billion. Today, the United States' national debt is over nineteen trillion dollars. This debt has been fueled not only by America's policy of stimulating the world economy through consumption on cheap credit, but also by the disappearance of a large portion of America's tax base through deindustrialization and overseas investments.[108]

The focus of this study has been on deindustrialization in the Midwest, but the South has not been exempted from deindustrialization. Deindustrialization is a national problem in America, and it needs to be addressed from a national standpoint. During and after World War II, the bulk of American defense industries were created or moved to the Sunbelt. Then during and after the Vietnam War, industries in the Sunbelt, such as textiles, apparel, and electronics, were in turn being reinvested overseas. The 1970's saw unprecedented disinvestment all across America and reinvestment overseas.[109]

The 1970s also witnessed an increase in mergers, acquisitions, and diversification. For example, U.S. Steel was investing 50% of its new capital investments into non-steel related industries, and was spending twice as much on replacing and upgrading non-steel related equipment than it was on steel plant upgrades. U.S Steel was buying everything from chemical firms to shopping malls. Two out of every three factories added to any one conglomerate's holdings during this period were due to the acquisition of an existing plant instead of investment in the building of a new plant. And most new plants were being built overseas. By 1976, 29% of U.S. imports for the year came from plants overseas that were a majority-owned subsidiary of an American multinational corporation. This development was unfortunate because it is a fact that American foreign investment destroys domestic jobs. Every $1 billion in foreign direct investment destroys roughly 26,500 domestic jobs, yet foreign direct investment increased sixteen fold between 1950 and 1980 from $12 billion to $192 billion. It is apparent that the actions of the financial sector and multinational corporations are destroying American jobs in order to enrich themselves, but pundits insist that this job destruction is a necessary casualty of progress towards a new post-industrial society in a global marketplace.[110]

The march towards globalization and the acquiescence of politicians has allowed international financiers and multinational banks to enrich themselves at the expense of the American worker. After the Great Recession, unemployment reached its highest level since the Great Depression, and those who are working are putting in longer hours and getting paid less money while CEOs are being paid more than ever. Profits for multinational corporations are at their highest ever, but American wages relative to corporate profits are at their lowest since the Great Depression. But these international financiers and multinational corporations are just taking advantage of an environment that was created by the politicians who were elected by the American people. The United States has effectively encouraged corporations to operate globally and shop around for the cheapest labor—and to build the infrastructure of potential rivals of the American worker—just to increase a profit margin.[111] In protest of the negative trends involved with globalization, Jon Jeter wrote:

> At the dawn of the twenty-first century, the United States is giving birth to the first generation of Americans whose life expectancy will be shorter, not longer, than their parents'. Our system of global finance has put us on the precipice, teetering on ruin. As of mid-2008, the United States has bequeathed to the world the biggest speculative bubble, the worst housing crisis, and the gravest economic meltdown in nearly eighty years, and the response from America's political class has been the largest single transfer of wealth from the poor to the rich in at least a century....Where there were factories, they have been made the vassals of kings like Wal-Mart, who can demand more and more work for less and less money. Gone are the days when a job at the factory provided a springboard to the middle class.[112]

The crisis of globalization can be easily seen in America's ever-increasing trade deficit, or in the massive bonuses received by traders on Wall Street in 2007 that amounted to more than $62 billion. Contrast these massive bonuses with how America's then elected officials charged almost $2,300 to every American man, woman, and child in order to bailout the international financiers. This has not been the result of the free market. It has been the result of policies implemented by American policy makers.[113]

For those who would speak out against the adoption of economic planning because it goes against the tenets of the free market, they should first note that America has been pursuing an economic plan ever since World War II. America's economic "plan" has consisted of a trade policy and a tax code that both encourage the exporting of American manufacturing overseas. This is a dangerous policy for both American industry and the American worker, and it is a dangerous policy for the security of the entire nation.

A Prescription for America

The two decades immediately following World War II were unprecedented in terms of economic prosperity for the United States. This prosperity was owed to the stimulus triggered by, not only fighting the war, but also by the post-war public investment in infrastructure. There was also the fact that America remained the only industrial nation spared from the destructive bombing campaigns that were utilized during the war. Because of America's unique economic position, business strategies developed a focus on maintaining short-term profits and keeping labor pacified. This business strategy has hurt workers and their communities, and has been detrimental to America's long-term prosperity and stability as a whole, especially when business leaders began taking advantage of tax codes to realize short-term profits via "paper entrepreneurship." "Paper entrepreneurship" is a term used by Edward J. Blakely and Philip Shapira that entails "the making of profits not from production but from buying and selling subsidiaries, asset stripping, write-offs, and real estate speculation."[114] In the new competitive global environment, flexibility to move in any direction that may be required is sought after, and the best way to ensure flexibility is to retain a high level of liquidity. The culmination of such greed-ridden practices occurred during the 1980s and can be witnessed in such notorious characters as the 1987 *Wall Street* movie villain, Gordon Gekko, who sought their fortunes through the acquisition of companies merely to shut them down and sell off their assets for quick cash with no regard for the effects upon a community or the nation as a whole.[115]

Yet, this practice would not be possible if it was not encouraged by a tax code that allowed acquisitions and mergers to be taken advantage of by large conglomerates. The United States tax codes offered incentives to merging and concentration by reducing the net cost of purchasing other companies. Mergers are essentially categorized as investment tax credits; thus, mergers or acquisitions have been given the same tax break as other forms of investment in capital. If the money or credit is available, then the purchase of another company took precedence over the building of a new plant because it was more profitable in the short-term. And the larger a conglomeration got, the easier it was to purchase other companies. Tax loopholes favored the largest and most profitable companies; thus, the tax code encouraged mergers and concentration. But the tax code also favored investment overseas over domestic investment. Overseas investment has been encouraged by a United States tax code that gave reduced tax rates to profits made overseas by American companies, and in many cases all taxes made overseas were not taxed until overseas profits were repatriated; thus, profits were perpetually reinvested overseas. The tariff laws also encouraged production overseas by offering loopholes for Domestic companies to assemble things overseas that were made in the United States and vice versa.[116]

In such a situation it is easy to see how an American company that is attempting to enter the European market could invest and move production overseas, close down the American plant, but still be able to sell in the American market because United States policy allows market access to its allies. There is a need to change federal tax codes and trade policies that offer loopholes and create incentives to close down domestic plants in order to move their production overseas.[117]

In *Plant Closings,* Richard B. McKenzie argued that planning at the national level to reverse deindustrialization would be detrimental to labor and industry. He asserted that restrictions on plant closings would prevent new industry from opening up and current industry from expanding. He further claimed that opposition to restrictions on plant closings is not pro-business, but pro labor because of its negative effect on long-term economic growth. However, McKenzie failed to realize that the issue is neither labor nor business oriented. Without a strong industrial base, America cannot sustain its global military dominance. This ultimately jeopardizes the security of every American. Even multinational corporations rely on the protections they receive under the American military umbrella. Besides, economic growth is undesirable if it only involves low-paying service jobs and a small handful of financial jobs at the top.[118]

Another industrial policy that McKenzie advises against in his critique of economic planning is bailouts. He argues that when the government interferes to rescue certain corporations—as it did in the cases of Chrysler, GM, and the bank bailouts—it serves only to "discourage firms, especially large, established ones that have the political muscle to attract the attention of the federal bureaucracy, from being attentive to their costs and revenues. To that extent, it will encourage business failures and will force many hard-working, lower-income taxpayers in this country to bail out many of their higher-paid colleagues in other industries. The justice of such a tax-subsidy arrangement must be called into question."[119] McKenzie is right in his assessment of large bailouts. However, spontaneous bailouts do not constitute a coherent national policy, but were merely used as a short-term fix to a long-term structural problem. The overhead structural problems need to be addressed, and they cannot be addressed simply by printing money and throwing it at the problem. A comprehensive approach to reversing deindustrialization needs to be implemented as an industrial policy at the national level.[120]

No reference to the auto bailouts should be made without the understanding that they were UAW bailouts by a Democratic president, which makes them a political favor to a specific constituency. Obama had an opportunity to reshape the underlying structural problems in the financial sector and in the auto industry. He had the opportunity to reverse the debilitating trends of deindustrialization and reinvigorate the auto industry to be a leader in green technology that could have reduced America's dependence on oil imported from hostile nations. He could have made the case for an American industrial policy that favored Americans, but politicians are beholden to international financiers and multinational conglomerates because they depend on campaign contributions from these entities.[121]

America should adopt an industrial policy that addresses the structural problems that have brought about deindustrialization across the United States. The issues of corporate profit squeezing needs to be addressed. Likewise, outsourcing and offshore production by American multinationals must also be addressed. Monetary policy, the tax code, trade policy, and deregulation for the finance sector all need to be integrated into a coherent whole as an integral part of any industrial policy prescription. In order to ascertain the best approach to dealing with these structural issues, various state and local strategies should be examined to find out which strategies might work the best on a national level.[122]

Generally, state and local strategies have taken threes strategies. The first strategy has been the investment in high-tech, financial, and service sector job creation, which represents a belief that the natural course of development is to move towards a post-industrial economy. Another method is to get rid of uncompetitive cost structures, such as labor, environmental regulations, and taxes, which result in measures against "big government" and unions to combat high pay and work regulations, an intrusive EPA, and high corporate taxes. The third strategy focuses on retaining the industries through employee stock ownership, industrial revenue bonds, and government aid in plant upgrades. Unfortunately, none of these strategies seem to tackle the overarching structural issues that are causing deindustrialization, but this is most likely due to the limited powers at the disposal of state and local actors.[123]

The alternative strategy must involve a comprehensive industrial policy that is implemented at the national level. This national policy needs to have the will to seriously reverse the trend of declining manufacturing and to reign in the hubris of the financial sector. In "Deindustrialization in the American Midwest: causes and responses," Ann R. Markusen and Virginia Carlson advocate an industrial policy that includes lower real interest rates for long-term investments, a capital fund for industry, a diversified R&D policy, and restrictions on mergers and financially-motivated corporate takeovers, which they believe would end paper entrepreneurship and encourage capital investments to remain at home. However, any serious industrial policy will also need to adopt reformation of the tax code and American trade policy in order to be truly effective.[124]

The Case for Economic Nationalism

Immigration

In 1973. in *The Coming of Post-Industrial Society*, Daniel Bell asserted that there were changes sweeping the industrialized world. He believed these changes proved the emergence of a knowledge-based economy that utilized technology and represented a new economy in contrast to the old outdated industrial one. However, deindustrialization was not a natural phenomenon that was meant to happen, nor did it just happen on its own. Deindustrialization has been the result of specific and conscious decisions by corporate executives that have based their decisions on American trade and tax policies. These policies were implemented by American policy makers at the national level. Plants were shut down and their production was relocated according to a corporation's private interest with no regard for America's local communities or the nation as a whole. Multinational corporations have based these plant closings on the most narrow of short-term economic considerations that benefit only a handful of investors, but their decisions have had long-term economic consequences for millions of Americans.[125]

Fifty years ago, permanent employment with the promise of a pension upon retirement was the standard in America. Now, temporary contracts that employ workers for either a few months or a few years has become the standard. American workers are left with only part-time work or temporary work because globalization has destroyed permanent work. There is no permanence because any one individual worker is completely interchangeable with another individual worker, which creates economic insecurity and insignificance that causes many of the unemployed to give up hope and drop out of the workforce. The unregulated free trade that is behind the push for globalization is closely tied to the agendas of multinational corporations and their preferences for a disposable labor force that is low-skilled and receives low-wages. Because politicians rely on campaign contributions from multinational corporations, they have pushed rhetoric of unrestrained free markets and open borders in order to undermine the protections that are necessary to ensure the economic security of the American people. Americans are finding it harder and harder to earn a decent living and to care for their families. Many Americans have no choice but to meander from one dead-end part-time job to another.[126]

Both the Democratic and Republican Parties have pushed the globalist agenda of multinational corporations and international finance at expense of the economic interests of the American people. Both political parties pursue agendas of international free trade that benefit multinational corporations and the finance sector over the interests of American workers. Both political parties advocate mass immigration that is advantageous to corporate elites but detrimental to the American workforce. Both political parties have betrayed America and the American people to globalist elites and foreigners.

The Democratic Party claims to stand for the economic interests of the poorest Americans with rhetoric that advocates a living wage for all Americans. However, raising the minimum wage does not increase the real wages of anyone because those added labor costs are passed on to consumers, which causes inflation of prices and leaves the minimum wage earner at the bottom of the economic ladder no matter how high the minimum wage is escalated. The only way to raise real wages is to shrink the labor supply. The Law of Supply and Demand demonstrates that the price of a resource only increases when the supply of that resource decreases relative to the demand for that same resource. Thus, the way to increase real wages is to decrease the supply of labor relative to the demand for labor. However, the Democratic Party openly advocates for open borders and increases in immigration, both legal and illegal, which can only increase the labor supply and decrease wages.[127]

The Republican Party has traditionally advocated for securing the border to prevent illegal immigration, but they pair this rhetoric with praise of legal immigration and even advocate for an increase in legal immigration. Whether immigration is illegal or legal has no impact on the Law of Supply and Demand and will increase the supply of labor relative to the demand for labor, which will cause a decrease in wages.

Calvin Coolidge, a hero of the Republican pantheon, identified protective tariffs and restrictive immigration as the main defenses against the international system, and stated so in his 1925 Inauguration speech. "Under the helpful influence of restrictive immigration and protective tariff, the rate of pay is high and wage-earners are in a state of content seldom before seen." Yet, the Republican Party of today advocates against both restrictive immigration and protective tariffs.[128]

Despite labor market research that has found that immigration hurts U.S. workers, immigration is welcomed by both major parties in the U.S. In a 2003 study, Harvard University economist George Borjas reported that increased immigration over the previous two decades had "substantially worsened the labor market opportunities faced by many native workers," reducing the wage of the average U.S.-born worker by 3 percent and the pay of high school dropouts by 9 percent. Such outcomes make economic sense; given a certain level of demand for labor, increased supply intensifies competition for jobs and exerts downward pressure on earnings. "By keeping labor supply down, immigration policy tends to keep wages high," writes economist Paul Samuelson in his classic textbook, *Economics*, commenting on restrictions on immigration in place until the mid-1960s.[129]

During the United States Senate Committee on the Judiciary on March 17, 2015 in reference to the H-1B visa program Senator Chuck Grassley of Iowa, the chairman of the committee, stated.

> The program was intended to serve employers who could not find the skilled workers they needed in the United States. Most people believe that employers are supposed to recruit Americans before they petition for an H-1B worker. Yet,

> under the law, most employers are not required to prove to the Department of Labor that they tried to find an American to fill the job first. And, if there is an equally or even better qualified U.S. worker available, the company does not have to offer him or her the job. Over the years the program has become a government-assisted way for employers to bring in cheaper foreign labor, and now it appears these foreign workers take over – rather than complement – the U.S. workforce.[130]

Studies show that H-1B visa workers are used as cheap labor to underbid and displace American tech workers. These foreign workers are imported en masse not because there is a lack of American tech workers, but because they work for lower wages than their American counterparts. In 2014, Disney laid off 250 tech workers and replaced them with foreign workers on H-1B visas. The same year, Southern California Edison laid off 400 tech workers who were also replaced by foreign workers on H-1B visas. And in both cases, the American workers being laid off were required to train their foreign replacements in order to receive their severance packages. These incidents had nothing to do with a shortage of qualified American tech workers, but are instead examples of cheap foreign labor being imported specifically to underbid and displace American workers.[131]

Since the opening of America to mass immigration via the

Immigration and Naturalization Act of 1965, real wages in the U.S. has decreased and the gap between the rich and the poor has widened. An increase in immigration has increased the domestic labor pool at the same time that deindustrialization and globalization have transferred millions of jobs overseas. While millions of Americans are unemployed or underemployed, foreign workers are given preference and brought in to fill newly created tech jobs or to displace Americans already in the tech industry. America needs to adopt an industrial policy to reverse deindustrialization, and it also needs to implement immigration restrictions in order to raise the real wages of native-born Americans.

Industrial Policy

Deindustrialization has been a widespread problem that threatens the entire nation; yet, all efforts to combat deindustrialization have been local community campaigns. State and federal resistance to deindustrialization has been largely non-existent. America should begin addressing deindustrialization at the national level through an industrial policy. An industrial policy needs to be a coordinated top-down approach to reverse the tide of deindustrialization. An American industrial policy should take into account and reconsider America's trade policy and ensure that the interests of the American people come before the interests of America's allies. The tax codes need to be reformed to permanently put an end to paper entrepreneurship and to encourage only those investments that promote the creation of capital and production of real value. The financial sector needs to be brought under control in order to serve the interests of America, rather than America serving the interests of the international financiers. An immediate moratorium on immigration, both legal and illegal, must be implemented along with mass deportations of third world migrant workers in order to shrink the labor pool, which would cause a real rise in wages and allow native-born Americans to obtain scarce jobs.[132]

America has fallen victim to a political and financial establishment that cares nothing for the economic prosperity of average Americans, the economic future of the American nation, nor the national security of America. Deindustrialization is not an incident from the past that has been weathered. Deindustrialization has continued up through today. Between 2000 and 2010, 23,000 factories shut down and more than five million manufacturing jobs were lost throughout the nation, which eliminated over $200 billion a year in payroll taxes. The Pentagon has noted concerns that America lacks the industrial capacity to fight a prolonged major war. World War II could not be won by the America of today. There is no more "sleeping giant," but a dead and dying relic of the past. Instead of producing what America needs, American imports continue to grow while exports shrink, and now America borrows enormous sums to pay for this trade imbalance. For example, more than a trillion dollars of American debt is owned by Japan and China alone. Currently, the victims of this system have been American industrial laborers and the middle class, but the day of reckoning for such irresponsible policies will soon be felt by every American.[133]

American policy makers are the ones responsible for placing the nation in such a precarious position. It has been their policies that have allowed and encouraged the deindustrialization that now threatens the nation's national security. Whether Democrat or Republican, policy makers represent their own interests, not the interests of the American people. These policy makers believe that borders are obsolete, they look to global networks for political power, and place global capital markets before the sovereignty of any one nation. It was an individual nation, the United States, which created these international markets through deregulation of the financial institutions, and America can regain its sovereignty by re-implementing regulations. Controls on foreign investment, currency speculation, the operation of multinational corporations, and tariffs can grant the United States its sovereignty back. However, whether left or right, political elites identify as internationalists who support globalization, and they care nothing for American jobs, nor do any of them genuinely identify with Middle America. They care nothing for average Americans; American causes are petty to such elites. International institutions, networks, and causes are placed before the priorities of the American people that they are supposed to represent.[134]

The biggest industrial employers in America are in the auto, steel, electronics, aircraft, and textile industries. These jobs also create markets for the service sector jobs and high technology jobs. They are also critical for American national interests because its defense systems depend on the steel, machine tools, auto, and aircraft industries. The loss of these industries and the jobs they support will also undercut the middle class. Tech jobs alone are not the answer because they depend on American industry for their customers. The tech sector's three biggest customers are GM, Ford, and Chrysler because computers are used to achieve better fuel economy, cleaner emissions, and better quality in cars. It would be difficult to imagine a Silicon Valley without a Detroit because multiple computers are utilized in the production of every new car. In order to preserve these vital industries, America needs an industrial policy.

The term “Industrial policy” scares people because it involves conscious and coherent, sustained, long-term planning. Americans want America to be strong, but they do not want to achieve that strength through economic planning. Americans want America to be strong by accident through capitalism, but the free market is not always efficient. Besides, industrial policy would not have to entail the end of the free enterprise system. The government should not pick winners and losers, but it needs to become more active in lifting up American industry to meet the challenges posed by foreign competition. Industrial planning does not equate to socialism. Americans need to get over the idea that planning will destroy capitalism because America is the only developed nation without an industrial policy. In 1987, Lee Iacocca proposed in an article, “Industrial Policy,” a six-point plan to define an American industrial policy that included:

1. The promotion of American energy independence by taxing foreign imports.
2. To provide specific limits to allies’ market share in the United States.
3. Give special education benefits to encourage high-technology fields of study.
4. Use incentives, such as tax-credits, to encourage research and development.

5. Implement a long-term program for rebuilding America's infrastructure.
6. And lastly, to force unions into making realistic concessions on wages and work rules that hamper efficiency.

Unfortunately, Iacocca's industrial policy was not taken seriously by American policy makers back then and deindustrialization has continued to undermine the economic well-being, as well as the national security, of America's future.[135]

Joel Blau, professor of social policy at Stony Brook University, believes the extension of democracy to industry and the workplace will renew the economic prospects of workers and give them a sense of control, which he calls "democratic accountability" in the economic sector. However, this would serve only to inhibit the future closing of already existent plants. Employee stock ownership may be right for some workers and for some communities, but an industrial policy for America needs to focus on changing the causes of deindustrialization and reversing it instead of merely attempting to slow it down. Thus, deindustrialization needs to be tackled from the national level.[136]

Nevertheless, before anything can be done, elitist policy makers must be held accountable to the American people instead of the international financiers and multinational corporations that they currently answer to. International causes need to be replaced with

American causes. America must become a nation that puts America and Americans first. Americans must become primarily producers rather than consumers. The current American trade deficit cannot continue indefinitely. The incessant borrowing of money from foreign governments is unsustainable. The divestment in America and the investment in foreign nations by American banks and corporations needs to come to an end. The outsourcing of American jobs overseas cannot be allowed to continue. Immigrant workers cannot be allowed to flood America and underbid American workers. Planning at the national level, via an industrial policy, is necessary if any of these aforementioned trends are to be reversed. Only those who are making a living through the systematic deindustrialization of America and globalization insist that planning is un-American and that unrestrained free trade is the only path to prosperity. But the average American has yet to witness any prosperity as a result of deindustrialization. Free trade proponents argue and assure that the reduction or outright elimination of impediments to free trade among nations can only increase global wealth and encourage peaceful international relations. Free trade, the power of global investors, the outsourcing of domestic manufacturing jobs, and the insourcing of foreign workers are all unpatriotic practices that have contributed to falling living standards. Furthermore, due to these unpatriotic practices, the gap between the rich and the poor in America has widened as wages for the average American continually shrink. America needs to pursue an economic policy that is beneficial to the American people. The American government is not accountable to the citizens of the world nor any other nation on this planet. The American government is accountable only to the American people.[137]

Conclusion

This study has presented the dire situation that globalization and deindustrialization have wrought on the United States. Traitorous politicians have forced a trade policy on America that leaves the American market open to competition from abroad, while allowing that same competition to keep American goods out of their respective domestic markets. This is not free trade; it is a disastrous and absurd trade policy. These politicians have shackled America with financial incentives and a tax code that encourages capital to be divested from domestic companies and reinvested overseas. These policies that cater to international financial and multinational corporate interests have caused widespread deindustrialization across America and have been disastrous for working class Americans. And while the average American is facing workplace displacement and decreasing wages, the politicians further their betrayal by important foreign competition, via immigration and H-1B visas, to compete with Americans in every field—whether they be low-skilled workers or high-skilled tech workers. The rules of the game have been stacked against the American people by the elected officials who are supposed to represent the American people, but instead serve only the interests of multinational corporations, international financiers, and foreigners at the expense of the American people.

The American people have been betrayed, but the nation as a whole has also been betrayed. The factories and industries that employed millions of Americans also built the armaments and weapons that fought our nation's wars. If a prolonged war was to erupt, then America would be forced to rely on foreign nations for the materials necessary to fight and win. This puts the national security of America in a precarious and dangerous position. Potential rivals and enemies of America cannot be relied upon during a time of war to provide the equipment necessary to prosecute a successful campaign of warfare. This is unacceptable and potentially damning for a nation that should be able to out produce any foreign adversary.

Globalization and deindustrialization have caused untold suffering for millions of Americans. Whole communities have been depopulated and left in a state of despair. Governments at the local, state, and federal level have accrued enormous debts dealing with displaced workers. The national debt has climbed to almost twenty trillion dollars, and an annual trade deficit of over five-hundred billion dollars has become the accepted norm. America is facing the first generation of Americans that can expect a bleaker economic future than their parents. The gap between the rich and the poor is the widest it's been since before World War II. Good paying manufacturing jobs have been replaced by low-paying service jobs that are part time, and the tech jobs that were supposed to replace low-skilled jobs are being handed over to foreign immigrants via H-1B visas. Nowhere is there respite for the working class, and the middle class is rapidly disappearing.

Americans have a right to be angry. American industry has not been wiped out because it was unable to compete. American industry has been wiped out because capital needed to modernize and increase productivity in domestic industry has been sent overseas to prop up foreign competition. Multinational corporations and international financiers made larger returns on their investments abroad due to tax codes and loopholes that encourage overseas investment. Whole industries that were profitable have been used as cash cows for overseas investment and then stripped of their assets and sold off to provide further capital for these overseas investments. The shifting of American industry abroad could have been prevented, but the United States government consciously pursued trade and financial policies that encouraged the outsourcing of production. And in order to bring production and jobs back to America, policies that favor domestic investment and production must be adopted at the national level.

An industrial policy needs to be embraced, not feared. Accusations that any such economic planning at the national level is socialism are completely unfounded. This type of rhetoric has been pushed by those elites who benefit from globalization, and they are the same elites who buy and own the politicians who have shackled America with such disastrous policies. Randian syllogisms have been fed to the American public, and free trade has been lifted up as an ideal by multinational corporations and international financiers who stand to benefit from such abstract idealism. America has never embraced free trade. America has historically pursued policies that benefit the American people and domestic business. Tariffs were once the main source of income for the federal government. Only recently have global elites began stripping America's protective barriers and spouting the doctrine of open markets. Keeping American markets wide open has not benefited America, but has instead coincided precisely with the demise of the American industrial base. Only the global elites stand to profit from open markets, and they have indeed profited at the expense of the American people.

Near the completion of this study, a champion of the American people has shifted the public debate to the very issues addressed throughout this study. This giant of American business has brought attention to the problems of deindustrialization and the plight of the American people. By sheer willpower and charisma, Donald Trump has brought to light the failed policies and trade deals made by the political establishment. Trump has challenged the prevailing political order that has brought ruin to American industry, and he has been crucified by the political establishment for addressing their charade. If Trump is not sabotaged by the global elites and their lackeys in Washington D.C. and the media, then he can "Make America Great Again" by reversing deindustrialization and bringing jobs back from overseas. The American people need a champion that is willing to put the welfare and prosperity of America first. The interests of the American people should come before the interests of multinational corporations, international financiers, foreign governments, and foreigners. The American people are not the pariahs of the world. Americans are industrial and innovative people, but they desperately need a government that works for their benefit. Make America for the Americans, and America will be great again.

Bibliography

Secondary Sources

Aamidor, Abe, and Ted Evanoff. *At The Crossroads: Middle America and the Battle to Save the Car Industry.* Toronto, Ontario: ECW Press, 2010.

Ann R. Markusen and Virginia Carlson. "Deindustrialization in the American Midwest: causes and responses," in *Deindustrialization and Regional Economic Transformation.* Edited by Lloyd Rodwin, and Hidehiko Sazanami. Winchester, Mass.: Unwin Hyman, Inc., 1989.

Blakely, Edward J. and Philip Shapira. "Public Policies for Industry." In *Deindustrialization and Plant Closure*. Edited by Staudohar, Paul D. and Holly E. Brown. Lexington, MA: D.C. Heath and Company, 1987.

Blau, Joel. *Illusions of Prosperity: America's Working Families in an Age of Economic Insecurity.* New York, NY: Oxford University Press, 1999.

Bluestone, Barry, and Bennett Harrison. *The Deindustrialization of America: Plant closings, community abandonment, and the dismantling of basic industry.* New York: Basic Books, Inc., Publishers, 1982.

Bluestone, Barry. "Deindustrialization and Unemployment," in *Deindustrialization and Plant Closure*. Edited by Staudohar, Paul D. and Holly E. Brown. Lexington, MA: D.C. Heath and Company, 1986.

Castree, Noel, Rob Kitchin, and Alisdair Rogers. "Enlightenment." In *A Dictionary of Human Geography.* Oxford, United Kingdom: Oxford University Press, 2013.

Cowie, Jefferson. *Capital Moves: RCA's Seventy-Year Quest for Cheap Labor.* New York: The New Press, 1999.

Davidson, Carl, and Steven J. Matusz. *International Trade and Labor Markets: Theory, Evidence, and Policy Implications.* Kalamazoo, MI: W.E. Upjohn Institute for Employment Research, 2004.

Davies, Phil. "Does Foreign Labor Hurt U.S.-Born Workers?" *Fedgazette* (October 2013): pg 10.

Dudley, Katherine Marie. *The End of the Line: Lost jobs, new lives in postindustrial America.* Chicago, IL: The University of Chicago Press, 1994.

Fabricant, Michael B. and Steve Burghardt. *The Welfare State Crisis and the Transformation of Social Service Work.* Armonk, New York: M.E. Sharpe, Inc.,1992.

Forman, Shepard. "America in Perspective: Major Trends in the U.S. Through 1990s," in *Diagnosing America: Anthropology and Public Engagement.* Edited by Shepard Forman. Ann Arbor, MI: University of Michigan Press, 1994.

Gottschalk, Peter and Mary Joyce. "The Impact of Technological Change, Deindustrialization, and Internationalization of Trade on Earnings Inequality: An International Perspective," in *Poverty, Inequality, and the Future of Social Policy: Western States in the New World Order.* Edited by Katherine McFate, Roger Lawson, and William Julius Wilson. New York: Russell Sage Foundation, 1995.

High, Steven. *Industrial Sunset: The Making of North America's Rust Belt, 1969-1984.* Toronto, CA. University of Toronto Press, 2003.

Hogan, Michael J. *The Marshall Plan: America, Britain, and the reconstruction of Western Europe, 1947-1952.* Cambridge, New York: Cambridge University Press, 1987.

Iacocca, Lee. "Industrial Policy."In *Deindustrialization and Plant Closure*. Edited by Staudohar, Paul D. and Holly E. Brown. Lexington, MA: D.C. Heath and Company, 1987.

Jeter, Jon. *Flat Broke in the Free Market: How Globalization Fleeced Working People.* New York, NY: W.W. Norton & Company, Inc., 2009.

Kletzer, Lori G.. "International Trade and Job Displacement in U.S. Manufacturing, 1979-1991." In *Imports, Exports, and the American Worker.* Edited by Collins, Susan M. Washington D.C.: Brookings Institution Press, 1998.

Lester C. Thurow. "Regional transformation and the service activities," in *Deindustrialization and Regional Economic Transformation.* Edited by Lloyd Rodwin, and Hidehiko Sazanami. Winchester, Mass.: Unwin Hyman, Inc., 1989.

Linkon, Sherry Lee, and John Russo. *Steeltown U.S.A.: Work and Memory in Youngstown.* Lawrence, Kansas: University Press of Kansas, 2002.

McKenzie, Richard B. *Plant Closings: Public or Private Choices?* Washington, D.C., 1984.

Meyer, David R. "Midwestern Industrialization and the American Manufacturing Belt in the Nineteenth Century." In *The Journal of Economic History,* 49 no. 4 (Dec., 1989): 921-937.

Miano, John "Low Salaries for Low Skills: Wages and Skill Levels for H-1B Computer Workers 2005," Center for Immigration Studies, 2007, http://www.cis.org/LowSalariesforLowSkills-H1B

Minchin, Timothy J. *Empty Mills: The Fight Against Imports and the Decline of the U.S. Textile Industry.* Lanham, Maryland: Rowman & Littlefield Publishers, Inc., 2013.

Newman, Katherine S. "Deindustrialization, Poverty, and Downward Mobility: Toward an Anthropology of economic Disorder," in *Diagnosing America: Anthropology and Public Engagement,* edited by Shepard Forman. Ann Arbor, MI: University of Michigan Press, 1994.

Nesvetailova, Anastasia. "Asian Tigers, Russian Bear and International Vets? An Excursion in the 1997-98 Financial Crises." *Competition and Change* 6, no. 3 (September 2002): pg 251-67.

Portz, John. *The Politics of Plant Closings.* Lawrence, KA: University Press of Kansas, 1990.

Russo, John and Sherry Lee Linkon. "Collateral Damage: Deindustrialization and the Uses of Youngstown," in *Beyond the Ruins: The Meanings of Deindustrialization.* Edited by Jefferson Cowie and Joseph Heathcott. Ithaca, NY: Cornell University Press, 2003.

Sachs, Jeffrey D. and Howard J. Shatz. "International Trade and Wage Inequality in the United States: Some New Results." In *Imports, Exports, and the American Worker.* Edited by Collins, Susan M. Washington D.C.: Brookings Institution Press, 1998.

Safford, Sean. *Why the Garden Club Couldn't Save Youngstown: The Transformation of the Rust Belt.* Cambridge, MA: Harvard University Press, 2009.

Shermer, Elizabeth Tandy. "Sunbelt Boosterism: Industrial Recruitment, Economic Development, and Growth Politics in the Developing Sunbelt." In *Sunbelt Rising: The Politics of Place, Space, and Region.* Edited by Michelle Nickerson and Darren Dochuk. Philadelphia, PA: University of Pennsylvania Press, 2011.

Steger, Manfred B. and Ravi K. Roy. *Neoliberalism: A very short introduction.* Oxford, United Kingdom: Oxford University Press, 2010.

Steger, Manfred B. *Globalization: A very short introduction.* Oxford, United Kingdom: Oxford University Press, 2013.

Stein, Judith. *Pivotal Decade: How the United States traded factories for finance in the seventies.* New Haven, CT: Yale University Press, 2010.

Stradling, David and Richard. "Perceptions of the Burning River: Deindustrialization and Cleveland's Cuyahoga River." Environmental History 13 (July 2008): pg 515-35.

Tillotson, Amanda. "Immigration Restriction as the Poor Man's Tariff: Lessons from the U.S., 1890-1925." *Conference Papers--Midwestern Political Science Association* (Annual Meeting 2009): pg 1-23.

Tuttle, Ian. "The H-1B Visa Program Gives American Workers a Raw Deal," *National Review,* August 3, 2015, http://www.nationalreview.com/article/421934/h-1b-visa-program-gives-american-workers-raw-deal-ian-tuttle

Walton, Gary M. and Hugh Rockoff. *History of the American Economy: Eleventh Edition.* Mason, Ohio: South-Western, Cengage Learning, 2010, pg 179, and McKenzie, Richard B. *Plant Closings: Public or Private Choices?* Washington, D.C., 1984.

Wilson, William Julius. *The Truly Disadvantaged: The inner city, the underclass, and public policy.* Chicago, IL: The University of Chicago Press, 1985.

"Detroit and Deindustrialization." *Dollars & Sense* no. 308 (Sept. 2013): pg 18-24.

"Encyclopaedia of Cleveland History," last modified: 30 March, 1998, http://ech.case.edu/cgi/article.pl?id=LT

"Encyclopaedia of Cleveland History," last modified: 30 March, 1998, http://ech.case.edu/cgi/article.pl?id=FBDOGMC

"Encyclopedia of Cleveland History," last modified: 13 May, 1998. http://ech.case.edu/cgi/article.pl?id=LSS

"GM News," accessed March 23, 2015,

http://media.gm.com/media/us/en/gm/company_info/facilities/assembly/dham.html

"H-1B visa," Wikipedia, accessed February 9, 2016, https://en.wikipedia.org/wiki/H-1B_visa#Criticisms_of_the_program

"How Do the Laws of Supply and Demand Affect the Labor Market?" accessed February 10, 2016, http://smallbusiness.chron.com/laws-supply-demand-affect-labor-market-58242.html

"Median Household Income in the United States," accessed March 18, 2015, http://www.davemanuel.com/median-household-income.php

"Restoring the American Dream," accessed April 7, 2015, https://www.gop.com/platform/restoring-the-american-dream/

"Western Reserve Historical Society," accessed January 5, 2015,

http://catalog.wrhs.org/collections/viewdocId=ead/MS4310.xml;query =Fisher%20Body;brand=default

"Western Reserve Historical Society," accessed January 5, 2015,

http://catalog.wrhs.org/collections/viewdocId=ead/MS4949.xml; chunk.id=bioghist_1;brand=default;query=republic%20steel

"Western Reserve Historical Society," accessed January 5, 2015,

http://catalog.wrhs.org/collections/viewdocId=ead/MS4950.xml; chunk.id=bioghist_1;brand=default;query=ltv

"U.S. National Debt Clock," last modified February 15, 2015. http://www.brillig.com/debt_clock/,

Primary Sources

Brazaitis, Thomas J. "The stench in steel." *The Plain Dealer,* October 30, 1977.

Chamberlain, Elmer G. "GM's Japanese connections attacked; is company exporting Ohioans' jobs?" *The Plain Dealer,* March 28, 1982.

Funk, Nancy. "USX strike is second in 27 years." *The Plain Dealer,* August 2, 1986.

Gerdel, Thomas W. "LTV Steel president moves up." *The Plain Dealer,* January 5, 1991.

Gerdel, Thomas W. "LTV rouses from dream of diverse empire." *The Plain Dealer*, May 26, 1991.

Grassley, Chuck. Prepared Statement by Senator Chuck Grassley of Iowa Chairman, Senate Judiciary Committee At a hearing entitled: "Immigration Reforms Needed to Protect Skilled American Workers" March 17, 2015

Kelly, Michael. "GM's strategy: Force UAW into concessions." *The Plain Dealer*, February 28, 1982.

Mahoney, Mike. "LTV trustee must dig out of legal paper avalanche" *The Plain Dealer,* July 19, 1986.

McCormick, Douglass. *The Cleveland Press*, February 26 1982. Fisher Body Coit Road Plant Collection: Container 1, Folder 18.

Rivera, Elaine. *The Cleveland Press*, February 27, 1982. Fisher Body Coit Road Plant Collection: Container 1, Folder 18.

Tabata, James. "Time to retaliate on Japan." *The Plain Dealer,* March 28, 1982.

Talbott, Stephen. "Steelworkers rally here." *The Plain Dealer,* December 3, 1986.

Taugher, Mary. *The Cleveland Press*, March 3, 1982. Fisher Body Coit Road Plant Collection: Container 1, Folder 18.

Sabath, Donald. "UAW can't save Coit Rd. GM plant." May 11, 1982. Fisher Body Coit Road Plant Collection: Container 1, Folder 18.

Sonfield, Matthew C. *The Impact of Foreign Competition on Selected American Industries.* Hempstead, New York: Hofstra University, 1985.

Sullivan, Elizabeth. *The Plain Dealer*, February 26 1982. Fisher Body Coit Road Plant Collection: Container 1, Folder 18.

Sullivan, Elizabeth."UAW leaders set strategy to get GM pact approved." *The Plain Dealer*, March 31.

Sullivan, Elizabeth. "Workers sick about GM's import venture." *The Plain Dealer,* May 26, 1982.

Sullivan, Elizabeth. "Global GM worries U.S. firms." *The Plain Dealer,* June 1, 1982.

Ungers, Jayne. *New-Herald,* February 26, 1982. Fisher Body Coit Road Plant Collection: Container 1, Folder 18.

Ungers, Jayne, "Domino Effect." *News Herald,* Fisher Body Coit Road Plant Collection: Container 1, Folder 18.

Associated Press. "Unions, unemployed seeking end to shutdown, job losses." *The Plain Dealer,* May 25, 1987.

Editorial in *The Plain Dealer*, March 25, 1982. Fisher Body Coit Road Plant Collection: Container 1, Folder 18.

Euclid Sun Journal, March 4, 1982. Fisher Body Coit Road Plant Collection: Container 1, Folder 18.

"Euclid plant workers approve GM contract." *The Plain Dealer*, April 5, 1982. Fisher Body Coit Road Plant Collection: Container 1, Folder 18.

Fisher Body Coit Road Plant Collection: Container 1, Folder 1.

"Here are GM commitments and UAW concessions." *United Press International*, April 9, 1982. Fisher Body Coit Road Plant Collection: Container 1, Folder 18.

U.S. Court of Appeals for the Third Circuit, No. 76-1749. Republic Steel Collection: Container 233, Folders 10-12.

U.S. Court of Appeals June 6th 1977 for the Sixth Circuit. Memoranda of Republic Steel Corp in Opposition to motion to require consolidation of subsequent filings by Petitioners. Republic Steel Collection: Container 229, Folders 7-21.

Youngstown Sheet & Tube Co. v. Sawyer, 343 U.S. 579 (1952).

Notes

1“Restoring the American Dream,” accessed April 7, 2015, https://www.gop.com/platform/restoring-the-american-dream/

2Lester C. Thurow. “Regional transformation and the service activities,” in *Deindustrialization and Regional Economic Transformation.* Edited by Lloyd Rodwin and Hidehiko Sazanami. Winchester, Mass.: Unwin Hyman, Inc., 1989., pg 188.

3“United States Balance of Trade,” Accessed February 10, 2016, http://www.tradingeconomics.com/united-states/balance-of-trade and “Jobs: The ‘Real’ Unemployment Rate Please? Anyone?” Accessed February 10, 2016, http://www.forbes.com/sites/dandimicco/2015/02/13/jobs-the-real-unemployment-rate-please-anyone/#6a22f53423d6

4Ann R. Markusen and Virginia Carlson. “Deindustrialization in the American Midwest: causes and responses,” in *Deindustrialization and Regional Economic Transformation.* Edited by Lloyd Rodwin and Hidehiko Sazanami. Winchester, Mass.: Unwin Hyman, Inc., 1989., pg 30.

5Ibid., pg 30.

6Ann R. Markusen and Virginia Carlson. “Deindustrialization in the American Midwest: causes and responses,” in *Deindustrialization and Regional Economic Transformation.* Edited by Lloyd Rodwin and Hidehiko Sazanami. Winchester, Mass.: Unwin Hyman, Inc., 1989., pg 31; Meyer, David R. “Midwestern Industrialization and the American Manufacturing Belt in the Nineteenth Century.” In *The Journal of Economic History,* 49 no. 4 (Dec., 1989): 921-937, 927.

7Ann R. Markusen and Virginia Carlson. “Deindustrialization in the American Midwest: causes and responses,” in *Deindustrialization and Regional Economic Transformation.* Edited by Lloyd Rodwin and Hidehiko Sazanami. Winchester, Mass.: Unwin Hyman, Inc., 1989., pg 31-5.

8Elizabeth Tandy Shermer. “Sunbelt Boosterism: Industrial Recruitment, Economic Development, and Growth Politics in the Developing Sunbelt.” In *Sunbelt Rising: The Politics of Place, Space, and Region.* Edited by Michelle Nickerson and Darren Dochuk. Philadelphia, PA: University of Pennsylvania Press, 2011, pg 33-8.

9Ann R. Markusen and Virginia Carlson. “Deindustrialization in the American Midwest: causes and responses,” in *Deindustrialization and Regional Economic Transformation.* Edited by Lloyd Rodwin and Hidehiko Sazanami. Winchester, Mass.: Unwin Hyman, Inc., 1989., pg 38-9.

10Ibid., pg 41-7.

11Ibid., pg 47-8.

12Barry Bluestone and Bennett Harrison. *The Deindustrialization of America: Plant closings, community abandonment, and the dismantling of basic industry.* New York: Basic Books, Inc., Publishers, 1982., pg

51-62.
13Sherry Lee Linkon and John Russo. *Steeltown U.S.A.: Work and Memory in Youngstown.* Lawrence, Kansas: University Press of Kansas, 2002., pg 134; Barry Bluestone and Bennett Harrison. *The Deindustrialization of America: Plant closings, community abandonment, and the dismantling of basic industry.* New York: Basic Books, Inc., Publishers, 1982., pg 63-6; Barry Bluestone. "Deindustrialization and Unemployment," in *Deindustrialization and Plant Closure.* Edited by Paul D. Staudohar and Holly E. Brown. Lexington, MA: D.C. Heath and Company, 1986., pg 6.
14Barry Bluestone and Bennett Harrison. *The Deindustrialization of America: Plant closings, community abandonment, and the dismantling of basic industry.* New York: Basic Books, Inc., Publishers, 1982., pg 63-6; Barry Bluestone. "Deindustrialization and Unemployment," in *Deindustrialization and Plant Closure.* Edited by Paul D. Staudohar and Holly E. Brown. Lexington, MA: D.C. Heath and Company, 1986., pg 6-7.
15Barry Bluestone and Bennett Harrison. *The Deindustrialization of America: Plant closings, community abandonment, and the dismantling of basic industry.* New York: Basic Books, Inc., Publishers, 1982., pg 63-6.
16"Detroit and Deindustrialization." *Dollars & Sense* no. 308 (Sept. 2013): pg 18-24.
17Ibid., pg 73.
18Ibid., pg 73-5.
19David Stradling and Richard. "Perceptions of the Burning River: Deindustrialization and Cleveland's Cuyahoga River." Environmental History 13 (July 2008): pg 529-30; "Encyclopaedia of Cleveland History," last modified: 30 March, 1998, http://ech.case.edu/cgi/article.pl?id=LT
20Jayne Ungers. "Domino Effect." *News Herald,* Fisher Body Coit Road Plant Collection: Container 1, Folder 18.
21Barry Bluestone and Bennett Harrison. *The Deindustrialization of America: Plant closings, community abandonment, and the dismantling of basic industry.* New York: Basic Books, Inc., Publishers, 1982., pg 67.
22Barry Bluestone and Bennett Harrison. *The Deindustrialization of America: Plant closings, community abandonment, and the dismantling of basic industry.* New York: Basic Books, Inc., Publishers, 1982., pg 67-9; Katherine S. Newman "Deindustrialization, Poverty, and Downward Mobility: Toward an Anthropology of economic Disorder," in *Diagnosing America: Anthropology and Public Engagement,* edited by Shepard Forman. Ann Arbor, MI: University of Michigan Press, 1994., pg 124.

23Timothy J. Minchin. *Empty Mills: The Fight Against Imports and the Decline of the U.S. Textile Industry.* Lanham, Maryland: Rowman & Littlefield Publishers, Inc., 2013., pg 306.
24Ibid., pg 306.
25Michael B. Fabricant and Steve Burghardt. *The Welfare State Crisis and the Transformation of Social Service Work.* Armonk, New York: M.E. Sharpe, Inc., 1992., pg 7-8.
26Katherine S. Newman. "Deindustrialization, Poverty, and Downward Mobility: Toward an Anthropology of economic Disorder," in *Diagnosing America: Anthropology and Public Engagement,* edited by Shepard Forman. Ann Arbor, MI: University of Michigan Press, 1994., pg 125.
27Ibid., pg 125.
28Peter Gottschalk and Mary Joyce. "The Impact of Technological Change, Deindustrialization, and Internationalization of Trade on Earnings Inequality: An International Perspective," in *Poverty, Inequality, and the Future of Social Policy: Western States in the New World Order.* Edited by Katherine McFate, Roger Lawson, and William Julius Wilson. New York: Russell Sage Foundation, 1995., pg 217.
29Ibid., pg 197.
30Katherine S. Newman. "Deindustrialization, Poverty, and Downward Mobility: Toward an Anthropology of economic Disorder," in *Diagnosing America: Anthropology and Public Engagement,* edited by Shepard Forman. Ann Arbor, MI: University of Michigan Press, 1994., pg 129-44; Peter Gottschalk and Mary Joyce. "The Impact of Technological Change, Deindustrialization, and Internationalization of Trade on Earnings Inequality: An International Perspective," in *Poverty, Inequality, and the Future of Social Policy: Western States in the New World Order.* Edited by Katherine McFate, Roger Lawson, and William Julius Wilson. New York: Russell Sage Foundation, 1995., pg 197-217.
31Shepard Forman. "America in Perspective: Major Trends in the U.S. Through 1990s," in *Diagnosing America: Anthropology and Public Engagement.* Edited by Shepard Forman. Ann Arbor, MI: University of Michigan Press, 1994., pg 1; Katherine Marie Dudley. *The End of the Line: Lost jobs, new lives in postindustrial America.* Chicago, IL: The University of Chicago Press, 1994., pg xix-xx, 30.
32Associated Press. "Unions, unemployed seeking end to shutdown, job losses." *The Plain Dealer,* May 25, 1987.
33"Western Reserve Historical Society," accessed January 5, 2015, http://catalog.wrhs.org/collections/view?docId=ead/MS4310.xml;query=Fisher%20Body;brand=default and "Encyclopedia of Cleveland History," last modified: 30 March, 1998, http://ech.case.edu/cgi/article.pl?id=FBDOGMC
34Bluestone, Barry, and Bennett Harrison. *The Deindustrialization of America: Plant closings, community abandonment, and the dismantling of basic industry.* New York: Basic Books, Inc., Publishers, 1982., pg

164-5.
35Ibid., pg 166.
36Ibid., pg 166-7, 183.
37Barry Bluestone. “Deindustrialization and Unemployment.” In *Deindustrialization and Plant Closure*. Edited by Paul D. Staudohar and Holly E. Brown. Lexington, MA: D.C. Heath and Company, 1987., pg 13-4; Barry Bluestone and Bennett Harrison. *The Deindustrialization of America: Plant closings, community abandonment, and the dismantling of basic industry*. New York: Basic Books, Inc., Publishers, 1982., pg 184; “GM News,” accessed March 23, 2015, http://media.gm.com/media/us/en/gm/company_info/facilities/assembly/dham.html
38Lori G. Kletzer. “International Trade and Job Displacement in U.S. Manufacturing, 1979-1991.” In *Imports, Exports, and the American Worker*. Edited by Collins, Susan M. Washington D.C.: Brookings Institution Press, 1998., pg 426.
39Ibid., 454-5.
40Barry Bluestone. “Deindustrialization and Unemployment.” In *Deindustrialization and Plant Closure*. Edited by Paul D. Staudohar and Holly E. Brown. Lexington, MA: D.C. Heath and Company, 1987., pg 10-11.
41Jayne Ungers. *New-Herald,* February 26, 1982. Fisher Body Coit Road Plant Collection: Container 1, Folder 18.
42Elmer G. Chamberlain. “GM’s Japanese connections attacked; is company exporting Ohioans’ jobs?” *The Plain Dealer,* March 28, 1982.
43Jayne Ungers. *New-Herald,* February 26, 1982. Fisher Body Coit Road Plant Collection: Container 1, Folder 18; Elmer G. Chamberlain. “GM’s Japanese connections attacked; is company exporting Ohioans’ jobs?” *The Plain Dealer,* March 28, 1982.
44Douglass McCormick. *The Cleveland Press*, February 26 1982. Fisher Body Coit Road Plant Collection: Container 1, Folder 18; Mary Taugher. *The Cleveland Press*, March 3, 1982. Fisher Body Coit Road Plant Collection: Container 1, Folder 18; Elaine Rivera. *The Cleveland Press*, February 27, 1982. Fisher Body Coit Road Plant Collection: Container 1, Folder 18.
45Elizabeth Sullivan. *The Plain Dealer*, February 26 1982. Fisher Body Coit Road Plant Collection: Container 1, Folder 18
46*Euclid Sun Journal*, March 4, 1982. Fisher Body Coit Road Plant Collection: Container 1, Folder 18; Elizabeth Sullivan. *The Plain Dealer*, February 26 1982. Fisher Body Coit Road Plant Collection: Container 1, Folder 18; Michael Kelly. “GM’s strategy: Force UAW into concessions.” *The Plain Dealer*, February 28, 1982.
47Editorial in *The Plain Dealer*, March 25, 1982. Fisher Body Coit Road Plant Collection: Container 1, Folder 18; “Median Household Income in the United States,” accessed March 18, 2015,

http://www.davemanuel.com/median-household-income.php
48Editorial in *The Plain Dealer*, March 25, 1982. Fisher Body Coit Road Plant Collection: Container 1, Folder 18.
49Elizabeth Sullivan. "UAW leaders set strategy to get GM pact approved." *The Plain Dealer*, March 31., 1982, and Editorial in *The Plain Dealer*, March 25, 1982. Fisher Body Coit Road Plant Collection: Container 1, Folder 18.
50" Euclid plant workers approve GM contract." *The Plain Dealer*, April 5, 1982. Fisher Body Coit Road Plant Collection: Container 1, Folder 18; "Here are GM commitments and UAW concessions." *United Press International*, April 9, 1982. Fisher Body Coit Road Plant Collection: Container 1, Folder 18.
51Donald Sabath. "UAW can't save Coit Rd. GM plant." May 11, 1982. Fisher Body Coit Road Plant Collection: Container 1, Folder 18.
52Fisher Body Coit Road Plant Collection: Container 1, Folder 1.
53Elizabeth Sullivan. "Global GM worries U.S. firms." *The Plain Dealer,* June 1, 1982.
54Elizabeth Sullivan. "Workers sick about GM's import venture." *The Plain Dealer,* May 26, 1982.
55James Tabata. "Time to retaliate on Japan." *The Plain Dealer,* March 28, 1982;
56Matthew C. Sonfield. *The Impact of Foreign Competition on Selected American Industries.* Hempstead, New York: Hofstra University, 1985., pg 320; James Tabata. "Time to retaliate on Japan." *The Plain Dealer,* March 28, 1982.
57Bluestone, Barry, and Bennett Harrison. *The Deindustrialization of America: Plant closings, community abandonment, and the dismantling of basic industry.* New York: Basic Books, Inc., Publishers, 1982., pg 126.
58Ibid., pg 118-26.
59John Portz. *The Politics of Plant Closings.* Lawrence, KA: University Press of Kansas, 1990., pg 2.
60Ibid., pg 3-10.
61"Western Reserve Historical Society," accessed January 5, 2015, http://catalog.wrhs.org/collections/view?docId=ead/MS4949.xml;chunk.id=bioghist_1;brand=default;query=republic%20steel
62"Encyclopedia of Cleveland History," last modified: 13 May, 1998. http://ech.case.edu/cgi/article.pl?id=LSS ; "Western Reserve Historical Society," accessed January 5, 2015, http://catalog.wrhs.org/collections/view?docId=ead/MS4949.xml;chunk.id=bioghist_1;brand=default;query=republic%20steel
63Funk, Nancy. "USX strike is second in 27 years." The Plain Dealer, August 2, 1986;

64Youngstown Sheet & Tube Co. v. Sawyer, 343 U.S. 579 (1952); "Western Reserve Historical Society," accessed January 5, 2015, http://catalog.wrhs.org/collections/view?docId=ead/MS4949.xml;chunk.id=bioghist_1;brand=default;query=republic%20steel

65"Western Reserve Historical Society," accessed January 5, 2015, http://catalog.wrhs.org/collections/view?docId=ead/MS4949.xml;chunk.id=bioghist_1;brand=default;query=republic%20steel

66Mike Mahoney. "LTV trustee must dig out of legal paper avalanche" *The Plain Dealer,* July 19, 1986; Stephen Talbott. "Steelworkers rally here." *The Plain Dealer,* December 3, 1986.

67Thomas W. Gerdel. "LTV rouses from dream of diverse empire." *The Plain Dealer*, May 26, 1991; "Western Reserve Historical Society," accessed January 5, 2015, http://catalog.wrhs.org/collections/view?docId=ead/MS4950.xml;chunk.id=bioghist_1;brand=default;query=ltv

68Thomas W. Gerdel. "LTV Steel president moves up." *The Plain Dealer,* January 5, 1991; "Western Reserve Historical Society," accessed January 5, 2015, http://catalog.wrhs.org/collections/view?docId=ead/MS4950.xml;chunk.id=bioghist_1;brand=default;query=ltv

69"Western Reserve Historical Society," accessed January 5, 2015, http://catalog.wrhs.org/collections/view?docId=ead/MS4950.xml;chunk.id=bioghist_1;brand=default;query=ltv

70Barry Bluestone and Bennett Harrison. *The Deindustrialization of America: Plant closings, community abandonment, and the dismantling of basic industry.* New York: Basic Books, Inc., Publishers, 1982, pg 142-3.

71Ibid., pg 145-7.

72Ibid., pg 149-52.

73U.S. Court of Appeals June 6th 1977 for the Sixth Circuit. Memoranda of Republic Steel Corp in Opposition to motion to require consolidation of subsequent filings by Petitioners. Republic Steel Collection: Container 229, Folders 7-21.

74U.S. Court of Appeals for the Third Circuit, No. 76-1749. Republic Steel Collection: Container 233, Folders 10-12.

75John Russo and Sherry Lee Linkon. "Collateral Damage: Deindustrialization and the Uses of Youngstown," in *Beyond the Ruins: The Meanings of Deindustrialization.* Edited by Jefferson Cowie and Joseph Heathcott. Ithaca, NY: Cornell University Press, 2003., pg 204; U.S. Court of Appeals for the Third Circuit, No. 76-1749. Republic Steel Collection: Container 233, Folders 10-12..

76Brazaitis, Thomas J. "The stench in steel." *The Plain Dealer,* October 30, 1977.

77Steven High. *Industrial Sunset: The Making of North America's Rust Belt, 1969-1984.* Toronto, CA. University of Toronto Press, 2003., pg 9; Sherry Lee Linkon and John Russo. *Steeltown U.S.A.: Work and Memory in Youngstown.* Lawrence, Kansas: University Press of Kansas, 2002., pg 131-4.
78Sherry Lee Linkon and John Russo. *Steeltown U.S.A.: Work and Memory in Youngstown.* Lawrence, Kansas: University Press of Kansas, 2002, pg 145.
79Ibid., pg 145.
80Jefferson Cowie. *Capital Moves: RCA's Seventy-Year Quest for Cheap Labor.* New York: The New Press, 1999., pg 4; Sherry Lee Linkon and John Russo. *Steeltown U.S.A.: Work and Memory in Youngstown.* Lawrence, Kansas: University Press of Kansas, 2002, pg 204-6.
81Sean Safford. *Why the Garden Club Couldn't Save Youngstown: The Transformation of the Rust Belt.* Cambridge, MA: Harvard University Press, 2009., pg 135-50.
82John Russo and Sherry Lee Linkon. "Collateral Damage: Deindustrialization and the Uses of Youngstown," in *Beyond the Ruins: The Meanings of Deindustrialization.* Edited by Jefferson Cowie and Joseph Heathcott. Ithaca, NY: Cornell University Press, 2003., pg 202.
83Ibid., pg 207-10.
84Richard B. McKenzie *Plant Closings: Public or Private Choices?* Washington, D.C., 1984., pg 8.
85Ibid., pg 3-8, 313.
86Gary M. Walton and Hugh Rockoff. *History of the American Economy: Eleventh Edition.* Mason, Ohio: South-Western, Cengage Learning, 2010, pg 179; Richard B. McKenzie *Plant Closings: Public or Private Choices?* Washington, D.C., 1984., pg 3.
87Manfred B. Steger *Globalization: A very short introduction.* Oxford, United Kingdom: Oxford University Press, 2013., pg 38-9; Noel Castree Rob Kitchin, and Alisdair Rogers. "Enlightenment." In *A Dictionary of Human Geography.* Oxford, United Kingdom: Oxford University Press, 2013.
88Carl Davidson and Steven J. Matusz. *International Trade and Labor Markets: Theory, Evidence, and Policy Implications.* Kalamazoo, MI: W.E. Upjohn Institute for Employment Research, 2004., pg 1-2,91.
89Jeffrey D. Sachs and Howard J. Shatz. "International Trade and Wage Inequality in the United States: Some New Results." In *Imports, Exports, and the American Worker.* Edited by Collins, Susan M. Collins. Washington D.C.: Brookings Institution Press, 1998., pg 239; Carl Davidson and Steven J. Matusz. *International Trade and Labor Markets: Theory, Evidence, and Policy Implications.* Kalamazoo, MI: W.E. Upjohn Institute for Employment Research, 2004., pg 21-7.

90Carl Davidson and Steven J. Matusz. *International Trade and Labor Markets: Theory, Evidence, and Policy Implications.* Kalamazoo, MI: W.E. Upjohn Institute for Employment Research, 2004., pg 18.
91Ibid., pg 99.
92Judith Stein. *Pivotal Decade: How the United States traded factories for finance in the seventies.* New Haven, CT: Yale University Press, 2010., pg 7.
93Michael J. Hogan. *The Marshall Plan: America, Britain, and the reconstruction of Western Europe, 1947-1952.* Cambridge, New York: Cambridge University Press, 1987., pg 427; Judith Stein. *Pivotal Decade: How the United States traded factories for finance in the seventies.* New Haven, CT: Yale University Press, 2010, pg 6-7.
94Judith Stein. *Pivotal Decade: How the United States traded factories for finance in the seventies.* New Haven, CT: Yale University Press, 2010, pg 8.
95Ibid., pg 5-8.
96Jefferson Cowie. *Capital Moves: RCA's Seventy-Year Quest for Cheap Labor.* New York: The New Press, 1999., pg 141l; Judith Stein. *Pivotal Decade: How the United States traded factories for finance in the seventies.* New Haven, CT: Yale University Press, 2010, pg 11-2.
97Judith Stein. *Pivotal Decade: How the United States traded factories for finance in the seventies.* New Haven, CT: Yale University Press, 2010., pg 122.
98Manfred B. Steger. *Globalization: A very short introduction.* Oxford, United Kingdom: Oxford University Press, 2013, pg 42-3; Manfred B. Steger and Ravi K. Roy. *Neoliberalism: A very short introduction.* Oxford, United Kingdom: Oxford University Press, 2010., pg 60; Judith Stein. *Pivotal Decade: How the United States traded factories for finance in the seventies.* New Haven, CT: Yale University Press, 2010, pg 35, 10, 117.
99Manfred B. Steger and Ravi K. Roy. *Neoliberalism: A very short introduction.* Oxford, United Kingdom: Oxford University Press, 2010, pg 31-3; Judith Stein. *Pivotal Decade: How the United States traded factories for finance in the seventies.* New Haven, CT: Yale University Press, 2010, pg 154.
100Anastasia Nesvetailova. "Asian Tigers, Russian Bear and International Vets? An Excursion in the 1997-98 Financial Crises." *Competition and Change* 6, no. 3 (September 2002): 253; Judith Stein. *Pivotal Decade: How the United States traded factories for finance in the seventies.* New Haven, CT: Yale University Press, 2010, pg 292-297.
101Bluestone, Barry. "Deindustrialization and Unemployment." In *Deindustrialization and Plant Closure.* Edited by Staudohar, Paul D. and Holly E. Brown. Lexington, MA: D.C. Heath and Company, 1987., pg 9-10.

102Judith Stein. *Pivotal Decade: How the United States traded factories for finance in the seventies.* New Haven, CT: Yale University Press, 2010, pg 119
103Ibid., pg 118-9.
104Ibid., pg 167.
105Manfred B. Steger. *Globalization: A very short introduction.* Oxford, United Kingdom: Oxford University Press, 2013, pg 48-53; Judith Stein. *Pivotal Decade: How the United States traded factories for finance in the seventies.* New Haven, CT: Yale University Press, 2010, pg 296-300.
106Michael B. Fabricant and Steve Burghardt. *The Welfare State Crisis and the Transformation of Social Service Work.* Armonk, New York: M.E. Sharpe, Inc., 1992., pg 6.
107Michael B. Fabricant and Steve Burghardt. *The Welfare State Crisis and the Transformation of Social Service Work.* Armonk, New York: M.E. Sharpe, Inc., 1992., pg 6-10; Judith Stein. *Pivotal Decade: How the United States traded factories for finance in the seventies.* New Haven, CT: Yale University Press, 2010, pg 6-8.
108"U.S. National Debt Clock," last modified February 15, 2015. http://www.brillig.com/debt_clock/, ; Michael B. Fabricant and Steve Burghardt. *The Welfare State Crisis and the Transformation of Social Service Work.* Armonk, New York: M.E. Sharpe, Inc., 1992., pg 9-12.
109Barry Bluestone and Bennett Harrison. *The Deindustrialization of America: Plant closings, community abandonment, and the dismantling of basic industry.* New York: Basic Books, Inc., Publishers, 1982., pg 33-40.
110Ibid., pg 40-6.
111Jon Jeter. *Flat Broke in the Free Market: How Globalization Fleeced Working People.* New York, NY: W.W. Norton & Company, Inc., 2009., xi- xix.
112Iid., pg xiii.
113Ibid., pg xv
114Edward J. Blakely and Philip Shapira. "Public Policies for Industry." In *Deindustrialization and Plant Closure*. Edited by Paul D. Staudohar and Holly E. Brown. Lexington, MA: D.C. Heath and Company, 1987., pg 140.
115Barry Bluestone and Bennett Harrison. *The Deindustrialization of America: Plant closings, community abandonment, and the dismantling of basic industry.* New York: Basic Books, Inc., Publishers, 1982., pg 118-26; Edward J. Blakely and Philip Shapira. "Public Policies for Industry." In *Deindustrialization and Plant Closure*. Edited by Paul D. Staudohar and Holly E. Brown. Lexington, MA: D.C. Heath and Company, 1987., pg 139-40.
116Barry Bluestone and Bennett Harrison. *The Deindustrialization of America: Plant closings, community abandonment, and the dismantling*

of basic industry. New York: Basic Books, Inc., Publishers, 1982., pg 126-33.
117Edward J. Blakely and Philip Shapira. "Public Policies for Industry." In *Deindustrialization and Plant Closure*. Edited by Paul D. Staudohar and Holly E. Brown. Lexington, MA: D.C. Heath and Company, 1987., pg 147.
118Richard B. McKenzie *Plant Closings: Public or Private Choices?* Washington, D.C., 1984., pg 310-11.
119Ibid., pg 312.
120Ibid., pg 312.
121Abe Aamidor and Ted Evanoff. *At The Crossroads: Middle America and the Battle to Save the Car Industry.* Toronto, Ontario: ECW Press, 2010., pg vii- ix.
122Ann R. Markusen and Virginia Carlson. "Deindustrialization in the American Midwest: causes and responses," in *Deindustrialization and Regional Economic Transformation.* Edited by Lloyd Rodwin and Hidehiko Sazanami. Winchester, Mass.: Unwin Hyman, Inc., 1989., pg 35.
123Ibid., pg 49-56.
124Ibid., pg 58.
125Steven High. *Industrial Sunset: The Making of North America's Rust Belt, 1969-1984.* Toronto, CA. University of Toronto Press, 2003, pg 7-8.
126Joel Blau. *Illusions of Prosperity: America's Working Families in an Age of Economic Insecurity.* New York, NY: Oxford University Press, 1999., pg xii- xiv, 43-4; Abe Aamidor and Ted Evanoff. *At The Crossroads: Middle America and the Battle to Save the Car Industry.* Toronto, Ontario: ECW Press, 2010, pg 372.
127"How Do the Laws of Supply and Demand Affect the Labor Market?" accessed February 10, 2016, http://smallbusiness.chron.com/laws-supply-demand-affect-labor-market-58242.html
128Amanda Tillotson. "Immigration Restriction as the Poor Man's Tariff: Lessons from the U.S., 1890-1925." *Conference Papers--Midwestern Political Science Association* (Annual Meeting 2009): pg 1-23.

129Phil Davies. "Does Foreign Labor Hurt U.S.-Born Workers?" *Fedgazette* (October 2013): pg 10.
130Prepared Statement by Senator Chuck Grassley of Iowa Chairman, Senate Judiciary Committee At a hearing entitled: "Immigration Reforms Needed to Protect Skilled American Workers" March 17, 2015

131Ian Tuttle, "The H-1B Visa Program Gives American Workers a Raw Deal," *National Review,* August 3, 2015, http://www.nationalreview.com/article/421934/h-1b-visa-program-gives-american-workers-raw-deal-ian-tuttle ; John Miano, "Low Salaries for Low Skills: Wages and Skill Levels for H-1B Computer Workers 2005," Center for Immigration Studies, 2007, http://www.cis.org/LowSalariesforLowSkills-H1B

132Steven High. *Industrial Sunset: The Making of North America's Rust Belt, 1969-1984.* Toronto, CA. University of Toronto Press, 2003, pg 12-7.

133Abe Aamidor and Ted Evanoff. *At The Crossroads: Middle America and the Battle to Save the Car Industry.* Toronto, Ontario: ECW Press, 2010, pg ix- xi.

134Manfred B. Steger. *Globalization: A very short introduction.* Oxford, United Kingdom: Oxford University Press, 2013, pg 65-6; Abe Aamidor and Ted Evanoff. *At The Crossroads: Middle America and the Battle to Save the Car Industry.* Toronto, Ontario: ECW Press, 2010, pg 371-2.

135Lee Iacocco. "Industrial Policy."In *Deindustrialization and Plant Closure.* Edited by Paul D. Staudohar and Holly E. Brown. Lexington, MA: D.C. Heath and Company, 1987., pg 54-6.

136Joel Blau. *Illusions of Prosperity: America's Working Families in an Age of Economic Insecurity.* New York, NY: Oxford University Press, 1999, pg 163-4.

137Manfred B. Steger and Ravi K. Roy. *Neoliberalism: A very short introduction.* Oxford, United Kingdom: Oxford University Press, 2010, pg 120; Manfred B. Steger. *Globalization: A very short introduction.* Oxford, United Kingdom: Oxford University Press, 2013.

Made in the USA
Monee, IL
04 November 2026

67380800R00095